T H E
HORSEMAN'S
ILLUSTRATED
DICTIONARY

Books by Steven D. Price

Essential Riding

The Quotable Horse Lover

The Kids' Book of the American Quarter Horse

The American Quarter Horse: An Introduction to Selection, Care, and Enjoyment

Caught Me a Big 'Un
(with Jimmy Houston)

The Ultimate Fishing Guide

The Polo Primer
(with Charles Kauffman)

Riding for a Fall

All the King's Horses: The Story of the Budweiser Clydesdales

Riding's a Joy
(with Joy Slater)

The Whole Horse Catalog
(with Barbara Burn, Gail Rentsch, Werner Rentsch, and David A. Spector)

Schooling to Show: Basics of Hunter-Jumper Training
(with Antonio D'Ambrosio Jr.)

Horseback Vacation Guide

Old as the Hills: The Story of Bluegrass Music

The Second-Time Single Man's Survival Handbook
(with William J. Gordon)

Take Me Home: The Rise of Country-and-Western Music

Get a Horse! Basics of Backyard Horsekeeping

Panorama of American Horses

Teaching Riding at Summer Camp

T H E
HORSEMAN'S
ILLUSTRATED
DICTIONARY

Steven D. Price

The Lyons Press

Printed in the United States of America

10 9 8 7 6 5 4 3 2 1

Library of Congress Cataloging-in-Publication Data

Price, Steven D.
    The horseman's illustrated dictionary/Steven D. Price
        p. cm.
    ISBN 1-58574-146-9
        1. Horses—Dictionaries   2. Horsemanship—Dictionaries   I. Title
    SF278.P75   2000
    636.1/003—dc21
                                            00-62147

Acknowledgments

Far too many people took the time and trouble over the years to explain horse words and phrases for me to express other than collective thanks. Far too many books revealed such words and phrases in texts and indices for me to list them. Suffice it to say that everyone who directly or indirectly contributed to this effort has the author's boundless gratitude.

However, one person cannot escape being singled out. Enrica Gadler, the editorial trail boss of this project, provided encouragement and expertise from start to finish, and with good sense and humor kept this maverick lexicographer on the right path.

Foreword

I believe there is much to learn from the title of a book. Many words mean different things to different people and there are a lot of phrases among horsemen that can bear likeness to a foreign language, especially to those not "in the know."

This book defines for everyone the horseman's language. If a stranger to the sport of horses should stumble across a group at a show, race, rodeo, or trail ride and not be savvy to their lingo, he could miss the point of the entire conversation. The words and phrases depicted in this illustrated dictionary truly enable everyone to understand what those horsey people are all talking about.

Throughout history, the horse has been man's companion. They have lived together, fought together, worked together and played together, producing a rich variety of words that have become an intrinsic part of our equine heritage. The horse, once a part of every family before being replaced by machines, is still an essential component of many individuals' lives. Today, there is that same desire to communicate with our horses. We talk to them, listen to them, and even carry on long conversations with them in our daily quest for a relationship.

The pleasure of the horse has taken on new forms and we now find ourselves in an era of specialization, creating the need for a greater understanding between those of different backgrounds or pursuits. It would be great if every horse enthusiast spoke the same universal language. Horses and those who care about them would find that with a standard vocabulary communication would be simplified. For the horse, confusion is always present when going from one handler to another; the same applies to the rider who decides to switch from English to Western or vice versa. So, when everyone understands the same words, it makes any transition easier for both, whether two- or four-legged.

Steve Price has put together a book not only for beginners but for specific equine groups to bridge the gap from one horse sport to another. He has compiled a great deal of information that allows newcomers and old timers to recognize the vocabulary of each other's interest in the horse world. It guarantees that reiners can understand jumper jargon and trail riders will feel right at home visiting with race horse enthusiasts. Hunter lovers won't be at odds with bull riders and ropers, cowboys can become fluent in dressage, and driving competitors can be privy to what the judges are looking for in Western pleasure.

This publication also gives the reader the opportunity to gain a working knowledge of different breeds of horses, their origins, needs and training methods, as well as descriptive horsemanship terms created by individual teachers. The reader will be able to readily identify the different tack or equipment used by various breeds or in individual riding styles and training techniques. This book explains the various horse show class titles and their specifications. In a short time one can become conversant with those who have learned the language from everyday use on the range, in the barn, or in the saddle shop or feed store.

If you were in a foreign land and someone gave you an animal that you had never seen or heard of before, one of the first questions you would ask might be, "What does it eat?" This volume furnishes much more detail than just answering your first query and the reading is easy, enjoyable, and very enlightening. Those of us who have been in the horse business all of our lives will find, when studying this book, that the old adage "what you learn after you know it all is what really counts," is a truism.

The Horseman's Illustrated Dictionary gives the reader an opportunity to learn several horse languages at once. Becoming proficient in horse related terminology will improve your understanding in many areas of the horse industry. As every golfer knows, when someone shouts "fore," it's time to duck, and likewise, when a horseman yells "heads up" a wreck is about to happen.

Steve Price has demonstrated his ability to take the complex and reduce it into simple terminology. This book fully illustrates the language of many great horsemen who are basically seat-of-the-pants riders and are far better at showing than telling. Many are not likely to verbalize what it is that they do; they just do it. In the past, the only avenue to learning was to watch. *The Horseman's Illustrated Dictionary* adds another dimension to the process, and you don't have to read between the lines. This book in reality speaks for the many great horsemen who had trouble putting words what they did or didn't do, giving the reader the words and meanings for all horse talk.

One of the greatest pleasures extended by working with horses is the opportunity to share knowledge. As you grow in knowledge, you will find yourself helping others to better understand this very unique animal we call the horse; you'll be able to pull up a bale of hay and chat with the best or horsemen, regardless of discipline. Even the slang expressions thrown out by those clever teachers are readily available in this guide. Those who thought a horn was something to blow or honk will learn how important it is to the Western rider. You'll discover that a coop does not necessarily contain chickens nor a coffin a body, and you'll concur with why some horsemen try to avoid the ominous "grob" (German for grave). Many who make their livelihood in the horse world cannot describe the "airs above the ground." There are some who don't know what a phaeton is, or its origin, or that a piggin' string has nothing to do with pigs. You'll wonder how an alligator could get loose in a horse arena and learn that a fender doesn't have to relate to your car. You will also find out that a ratcatcher is not on the endangered species list and that an elevator goes neither up nor down but fits in a horse's mouth. And, when horsemen talk about the bottom line, don't look for it at the end of your financial statement.

The Horseman's Illustrated Dictionary contains a wealth of knowledge and should be in the library of anyone remotely interested in this most athletic animal. Learning is a never-ending process, and I'm sure this publication will pique your interest in exploring all the aspects of the world of horses.

Don Burt

Introduction

My favorite summer job during my college years was teaching riding at a summer camp. My second favorite was working on a dictionary.

The work in question, *The Random House Dictionary of the English Language,* was being compiled under the supervision of a family friend who headed Random House's College and Reference Department (I got my job through unabashed nepotism). My task, in those precomputer days, was to alphabetize index cards. Newspaper and magazine readers from all over the country clipped out examples of newly coined words, pasted them onto index cards and mailed them in by the shoeboxload. The idea was to monitor the frequency with which these neologisms appeared in print with regard to whether any should be included in the dictionary.

Giving myself the grandiose title of Lexicographical Systematizer and spending a disproportionate amount of take-home pay on Murine and Visine, I alphabetized shoebox after shoebox of three-by-five-inch index cards. I began to feel like the Sorcerer's Apprentice. It was a good thing I liked words.

As the line from *H.M.S. Pinafore* goes, I polished up the handle so carefully that I was invited back the following summer. And I was promoted: in addition to alphabetizing the cards, I was invited to write definitions. My categories were heraldry and falconry, rather esoteric subjects but what else would you give to an English Lit major who was there only for the summer?

Writing definitions began by my poring through reference books for information, then preparing an as clear and as all-encompassing definition of the word or phrase that I could devise. The editor who reviewed my work taught me much about the art and craft of concise and comprehensive—and especially, useful—writing. It was a marvelous summer, admittedly not nearly so exciting as riding horses six hours a day, but not a bad way for a college English major to learn vital aspects of the writing craft.

As I compiled this horseman's dictionary, I recalled what I had learned those many summers ago, especially with regard to usefulness. Words and phrases are presented in the context of how the reader would come across them, whether while taking a riding lesson (*wrong lead, hold out,* or *crest release*), spectating at an equestrian event (*trifecta, working cow horse,* or *clear round*), overhearing experienced horsemen chatting (*weedy, rub on,* or *covert*) or reading a horse-related book or magazine or a tack shop catalog (Spanish Riding School, Coggins Test, or *full-cheek snaffle*).

I also included word derivations when they were of particular interest. For example, *canter* comes from the gait at which Chaucer's *Canterbury Tales* pilgrims traveled along their loquacious way, *phaeton* is named for the son of a Greek god, and *bug boy* refers to the insect-looking asterisk beside the name of an apprentice jockey as listed in the racetrack's program.

Every activity has its esoteric vocabulary, and horse sports and the industry that supports the sports are no exception. Some words mean nothing to outsiders (*renvers, latigo, chukkar*). Others mean one thing to outsiders, but quite another to the horse world (*leak, near, hock*). In that spirit, this reference is meant to provide a useful working vocabulary for just about every aspect of horse use and care. To keep the book from becoming unwieldy in size and overly technical, I exercised the compiler's right of selectivity; the reader who is interested in more information about veterinary matters is directed to any of the many books devoted to horse health.

Although every effort was taken to make this book as accurate as possible, if an error of fact or judgment slipped in, let me apologize in the spirit of Samuel Johnson: When asked how he came to define *pastern* in his dictionary as "the knee of a horse," Johnson replied, "Ignorance, Madam, pure ignorance."

Steven D. Price
New York, NY
July 2000

THE
HORSEMAN'S
ILLUSTRATED
DICTIONARY

above the bit

The position of a horse that is holding his head above the rider's hands, done to evade the effects of the bit. *See also* on the bit, behind the bit.

Horse's head above the bit

(©CHERRY HILL)

above the ground

See airs above the ground.

acey-deucy

In racing, stirrups adjusted so the inside one is lower than the outside one, in order to give the jockey better balance while riding around turns.

across the board

In racing, one wager to win, place, and show (in effect, three bets in one). If the chosen horse finishes first, the ticket holder receives the win, place, and show payoffs. If the horse finishes second, payoff is for place and show; if third, for just show.

action

The elevation of a horse's legs, especially with regard to knees and feet. The animatedly high action of a Saddlebred or Tennessee Walking Horse contributes to the breed's showiness, while the low, daisy cutter action of a show hunter's trot is valued for its ability to cover ground at each stride.

add a stride
To increase by one the number of strides between two jumps, done by the rider's shortening the horse's stride. *See* leave out a stride.

added money
In racing, money added to a purse, often by the track or a sponsor, in addition to nominations and entry fees.

Adult Amateur
A category of horse show classes open to amateur riders over the age of eighteen. *See* Amateur Owner.

advanced
The highest level of competition in combined training and dressage events.

aged
A horse that is four years or older. *See also* senior.

aging
The process of determining a horse's age from tooth size, shape, and markings. Permanent incisor teeth appear before the age of five; cuplike indentations in the incisors disappear by eight; the tops of incisors change from rectangular to triangular by fifteen years, at which time Galwayne's groove appears on the third incisor and extends the length of the tooth by age twenty.

From left to right: A horse's teeth at five, seven, and twenty years of age

(© CHRISTINA BERUBE)

ahead of the motion
See motion.

aid
A command signal from the rider to the horse. The natural aids are leg pressure, rein pressure, and the weight of the rider's seat. Artificial aids, which reinforce the natural aids, include the spur and the whip. *See also* cue.

airs
Certain advanced movements in classical horsemanship, such as the piaffe, passage, Spanish walk, and the airs above the ground.

airs above the ground
the movements in which two or more of the horse's feet leave the ground, such as the levade, capriole, and courbette. These so-called high school movements (from the French *haute école*) are said to have come from the requirement during the late Middle Ages and Renaissance that a mounted warrior's horse act as both an offensive weapon and a shield. A rearing horse could disable an opponent or his steed while also stopping a sword or spear thrust directed at the rider.

An Akhal-Teke stallion

(© LINDA AARON / AKHAL-TEKE
ASSOCIATION OF AMERICA)

Akhal-Teke

A breed of Russian sport horse that originated in present-day Turkistan (north of Iran). It has a fine solid-colored coat with a metallic sheen, stands on relatively long and slender legs, and reaches a height of about 15.2 hands. Possessing great stamina, the Akhal-Teke is used for racing in its native region and for endurance riding: in 1935, Akhal-Tekes were ridden from Turkistan to Moscow, some twenty-five hundred miles (including six hundred miles of desert) in eighty-four days.

Al Barak

In Islamic legend, the milk-white mare that conveyed Mohammad from Earth to heaven. She had the wings of an eagle and a human face. Every one of her strides was equal to the farthest range of human sight.

alfalfa

A nutrient-rich legume widely used for hay.

all-around champion

In Western horse shows, the contestant who wins the most aggregate points in all events in which he takes part; in rodeos, the winner of the most aggregate money in all such events.

alligator

In cutting, a difficult cow that makes every effort to escape back to the herd.

allowance race

In racing, a race in which eligibility is based on amounts of money won or the number of races won over a specified time.

also eligible

In racing, a horse that is officially entered but not permitted to start unless the field is reduced by scratches.

also-ran

In racing, a horse that did not finish first, second, or third.

amateur

One who rides or drives horses without receiving compensation (as distinguished from a professional). *See also* nonpro.

Amateur Owner

A horse show class open to horses that are ridden by their adult owners or a close adult relative of the owner.

Amazone

An obsolete term for a female rider or driver.

amble

The slow form of the pace, approximately the speed of a jog or slow trot. Not all horses can amble; the gait is performed naturally by Standardbreds, Tennessee Walking Horses, and several other breeds to whom lateral gaits come naturally. Horses that ambled were especially valued for their comfortable gait in the centuries before riders discovered posting.

American Cream Draft

The only draft breed to originate in the United States, the American Cream Draft is descended from "Old Granny" whose foaling date has been placed between 1900 and 1905. The horses are a medium cream color with white mane and tail, pink skin and amber eyes. Height ranges from 15.1 to 16.3 hands; weight between 1,600 and 2,000 pounds. The American Cream Draft is used for agricultural work and for showing.

American Horse Council

An equine trade association that is especially active in federal and state legislation involving horses, headquartered in Washington, D.C.

American Horse Shows Association

The national federation and regulatory body of horse sports in the United States, headquartered in Lexington, Kentucky.

American Quarter Horse

The most populous breed of horses in the world, noted for their quick bursts of speed (the name comes from the ability to run one-quarter of a mile faster than any other breed). The breed originated during the colonial era in America after a Thoroughbred named Janus was bred to native mares; their offspring possessed the ability to cover short distances at great speed. Quarter Horses went west with the settlers, where their speed and agility made them useful for cattle ranching. Many were crossed with descendants of the horses brought over by Spanish settlers in Mexico and the American southwest and with wild mustangs, all of which added to the hardy stock.

American Quarter Horses ("American" was added to the breed's name in 1940) are characterized by a compact shape, strong hindquarters, and a quiet sensible temperament. They are now used for ranching, West-

American Quarter Horse

(© D.R. STOECKLEIN/AMERICAN QUARTER HORSE ASSOCIATION)

ern (and some English) horse showing, Quarter Horse racing, and pleasure riding.

American Saddlebred

A breed of horses used as three- and five-gaited riding horses and for fine harness driving. Created by crossing pacers with Morgans and Thoroughbreds, the breed was popular throughout the southern states in the nineteenth century as an animated yet comfortable riding horse. With their arched necks and elegant bodies, Saddlebreds are now used primarily as show horses; their high-stepping walk, trot, and canter (and in the case of five-gaited horses, their slow gait and rack) prompt enthusiastic cheers from spectators. *See also* saddle-seat equitation.

Andalusian

The native breed of Spain, created by crossing the Barb and Arab with heavier types. These horses helped create classical horsemanship centuries ago; the first horses at Vienna's Spanish Riding School came from Spain (hence the establishment's name). Standing at about 15.2 hands high, the Andalusian has a well-muscled body that lends itself to dressage and trail riding.

Anglo-Arab

The term for a crossbred between a Thoroughbred sire and Arabian dam, used for foxhunting, jumping, and pleasure riding.

ankle boots

Coverings for the hind fetlock joints as protection against brushing. *See* brushing.

A three-gaited American Saddlebred in the showring

(© SARGENT/AMERICAN
SADDLEBRED HORSE ASSOCIATION)

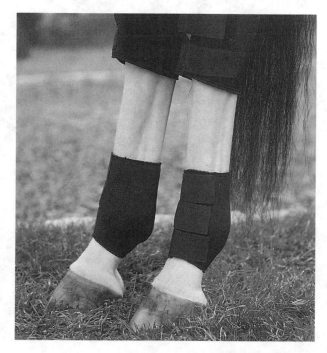

Ankle boots

(© MILLER HARNESS COMPANY L. L. C.)

anticast roller

A surcingle with a metal prong that presses uncomfortably against the horse's back when the animal rolls. Its purpose is to discourage horses that have a tendency to become cast from lying on their backs. *See* cast.

antigrazing rein (or device)

A strap running from the saddle through the browband and attaching to the bit, to prevent the horse from grazing and, in the process, pulling the rider over his head.

Antigrazing rein becomes taut when the horse lowers his head

(© MILLER HARNESS COMPANY L. L. C.)

Blanket-patterned Appaloosa

(© DON SHUGART / APPALOOSA HORSE CLUB)

Appaloosa

A breed developed in the eighteenth century by the Nez Percé tribe of Native Americans and named for the Palouse River region of Idaho, Oregon, and Washington. The breed is easily recognizable by the spotted "blanket" over its rump (although leopard Appaloosas have spots all over their bodies), which the Nez Percé believed had magical qualities. Appaloosas also have striped hooves and a white sclera around the pupil of the eye. They can be found doing ranch work, competing in Western horse shows, and as jumpers and pleasure mounts.

Appendix Registry

The section of the American Quarter Horse Association registry for horses that are American Quarter Horse-Thoroughbred crossbreds.

appointments

Saddlery and harness when worn by horses and ponies. In a horse show appointments class, the appropriateness and condition of these items are judged.

apprentice

In racing, a jockey who is just beginning his or her career. In handicapped races, apprentices receive weight allowances: until they have won ten races, they carry ten fewer pounds, seven fewer pounds from eleven to fifteen wins, and five fewer pounds from the thirty-fifth win until one year from the date of the victory. This system provides an incentive for trainers to give unproven jockeys a chance to ride.

Apprentice allowances are indicated in racetrack programs by one or more asterisks (*). Because the asterisk resembles an insect, apprentices are known as bug boys.

apron

(1) the skirt of a sidesaddle habit;.

(2) in driving, a protective cloth wrap worn around the driver's waist to keep dirt off his or her clothing.

Arabian

The breed that has been the foundation stock of all light breeds and itself acknowledged to be the world's oldest breed. The Arab—the breed is the Arabian; a member of the breed is an Arab—is characterized by a dish-shaped convex head with a forehead bulge called the jibbah, fine body features, and a high tail-carriage. Its skeletal structure is unique among horses: seventeen ribs, five lumbar bones and sixteen tail vertebrae (as compared with eighteen, six, and eighteen in other breeds and types).

Beginning in the seventeenth century, these so-called desert horses were imported from the Middle East and North Africa into Europe and then to America. Their ability to pass along their speed and endurance, as well as their fine looks and docile temperament led to widespread crossbreeding. Almost every modern breed can trace a portion of its bloodlines to the Arabian, most notably the Thoroughbred, Andalusian, and Lipizzaner.

The four most prominent strains of Arabians are the Polish, the Egyptian, the Spanish, and the Russian. Supporters of each group carefully maintain the purity of the lines through selective breeding.

Because of the ease with which they can travel long distances over the most rugged terrain, Arabians excel at endurance and competitive trail riding. They are also raced, used as pleasure riding horses, and shown in Western and English classes. Some of the most

Arabian

popular events at an all-Arabian show are Native Costume classes, in which horses and riders wear authentic or fanciful Bedouin tack and attire.

arena polo
Another name for indoor polo, which is played in a covered arena. In contrast to the outdoor version, three players constitute a team, six chukkars of seven minutes each comprise a match, a rubber ball is used instead of one made of solid wood, and the goalposts are painted on the sideboards at the ends of the arena. *See* polo.

artificial aid
The spur or the whip, used to reinforce the natural aids (leg, hands, seat, and voice). *See* aid.

artificial insemination
Manually implanting a mare with semen that has been collected from a stallion, as distinguished from a cover, or live, breeding.

ascarid (ASS-kar-id)
A parasitic roundworm that, when ingested as eggs during grazing, causes diarrhea, colic, and other internal problems. Ascarids can be both prevented and treated with worming medication.

ass
An equine species that originated in central Asia and Africa. Characterized by a small (approximately thirteen hands high) chunky body and longer ears than horses have, the wild ass and its cousin the onager were crossed with horses and ponies. The result was the domesticated ass, of which the donkey is the best-known member of that family. Because domesticated asses do not thrive in severely cold and damp climates, they are most prevalent in Mediterranean and South American regions for use as pack animals and for riding.

automatic waterer (or fountain)
A stall fixture that supplies drinking water and automatically refills the basin whenever the water level drops below a certain point. Because a horse's water intake cannot be monitored by the use of such a device, many horsemen prefer to use hand-filled buckets.

auxiliary starting gate
In racing, a second starting gate used when the number of horses in a race exceeds the capacity of the main starting gate (which usually hold twelve horses).

azoturia
Severe muscle cramping in the small of the back caused by the buildup of lactic acid in the muscle. The condition is characterized by a stiff, wobbling walk and trot and by dark-colored urine. It is often seen in horses that have eaten protein-rich feed on rest days following exercise. Azoturia is familiarly known as Monday-morning disease because horses that rested following exertion over weekends came down with it. It is rarely seen nowadays, thanks to proper stable management and care.

back
(1) to cause a horse to step or walk backward, also known as rein-back;
(2) to introduce a horse to being ridden;
(3) in polo, the player whose primary function is to defend his team's goal.

back at the knee
See calf-kneed.

back cinch
The rear girth of a Western saddle. The second cinch adds extra security during strenuous activities such as roping.

back fence
In a cutting competition, the part of the fence directly behind the herd. If the cow being worked is allowed to reach any part of the back fence, the horse will lose points.

Back cinch

(© CHERRY HILL)

backhand
In polo, a stroke that sends the ball behind the player.

backside
The colloquial word for a racetrack's stable area.

backstretch
The far side of an oval racetrack, the side opposite the finish line.

Badminton
A major international horse trial held in the spring on the Gloucestershire, England, estate of the Dukes of Beaufort (which also gave its name to the racquet sport of Badminton). Started in 1949, it ranks with Burleigh, Lexington, and the Olympics as one of the world's most demanding three-day events.

Baker blanket
A blanket held in place by straps that cross under the horse's belly. Designed by the late horse show trainer D. Jerry Baker.

Balanced seat

balanced seat
The standard position in which the rider's upright upper body remains over the horse's center of balance at all gaits. By far the most prevalent style of riding, it acquired its name in the early twentieth century to distinguish between it and the forward seat.

bald
A wide, white facial marking that extends from forehead to nostrils, usually covering one or both eyes.

balding girth
A leather girth with a contoured shape designed to prevent chafing the skin of the horse's elbow.

ball
A large medicine pill for horses, given orally by means of a balling gun, a large syringelike device that forces the pill down the horse's throat.

ballotade
An air above the ground, a variation of the capriole, in which the horse leaps off the ground with the soles of his hind feet visible from the rear. *Cf.* croupade.

bangtail
A slang expression for a horse whose tail has been made shorter by being cut straight across, usually at hock level.

bank
A jumping obstacle composed of a natural or artificial mound of earth that, depending on the course, the horse and rider jumps onto or off. In some parts of the world where timber

to make fencing was scarce, fields were separated by series of banks and ditches (the earth scooped up to make the ditches became the banks); the banks became the inspiration for such showring obstacles.

bar

(1) The space between the horse's incisors and lower molar teeth that accommodates the bit; (2) The part of the hoof between the toe and heel.

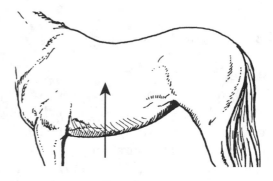

Barrel

barrel

The midsection of a horse, between the forelegs and the loins.

barrel racing

A timed Western horse show and rodeo event in which riders maneuver around three barrels in a cloverleaf pattern. It originated strictly as a sport (that is, without any practical ranching antecedents). Although events are open to both men and women, barrel racing is almost exclusively done by women.

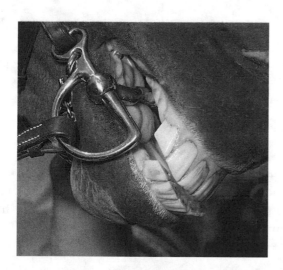

Placement of the bit in the horse's bar
(© MILLER HARNESS COMPANY L. L. C.)

Barb

A native North African breed similar to the Arab although with slightly coarser features and without the dish face. Native to the Barbary States, once a North African confederation, the breed was imported into Europe where, like the Arabian, it contributed to the formation of the Thoroughbred, Adalusian, and other breeds. *See also* Godolphin Barb.

barley

A cereal grain used as feed.

Barrel racing competition
(© AMERICAN QUARTER HORSE ASSOCIATION)

barren
Of a mare, unable to conceive.

barrier
In roping, a cotton or elastic rope or a photo-electric device in front of the calf's and the roping horse's starting boxes. The barriers are released to make sure the calf gets a head start; if the horse breaks the barrier before it is released, penalty seconds will be added to the roper's time.

bar shoe
A type of horseshoe that has a strip of metal across its width. Because the bar prevents the foot from spreading, such shoes are typically used on feet that need extra support.

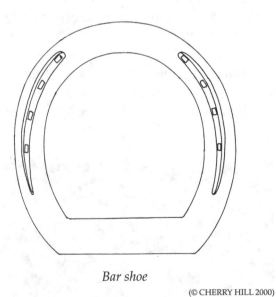

Bar shoe

(© CHERRY HILL 2000)

bascule
The smooth arc of the horse's body, from poll to croup, over a jump. The word is French meaning "smooth bend."

bat
A short crop with a wide tab end, used primarily in racing or jumping.

Baucher, François [1796–1873]
French horseman, instructor, and trainer. He spent much of his career applying dressage to the training of circus horses and to cavalry mounts.

bay
A body color ranging from dark to light brown and always with a black mane and tail and usually black markings on the lower legs.

bearing rein
See neck rein.

beat
The number of footfalls at a gait. The walk is a four-beat gait, the trot has two beats, and the canter or lope has three.

bedding
A cushion layer with which stall and trailer floors are covered for comfort and to absorb moisture. Wood shavings and straw are the most popular choices.

behind the bit
The position of a horse that has lowered or overflexed his head in order to evade the effects of the bit. Also called "below the bit."

behind the motion
See motion.

Horse holding his head behind the bit
(© CHERRY HILL)

Belgian

A draft breed that originated in Belgium, a descendant of the medieval Flemish War Horse (which also contributed to the Clydesdale and Shire draft breeds). Standing approximately seventeen hands high and almost always roan or chestnut in color, the Belgian has a deep barrel and strong shoulders and back. Like other draft breeds, it is used for hauling and agricultural work.

bell boot

A rubber boot worn on the front ankle to protect against overreaching.

Belmont Stakes

The final race of the Triple Crown, a distance of one and a half miles, held at Belmont Park in New York City three weeks after the Preakness.

bench-kneed

A conformation fault characterized by knees that are set to the outside of the cannon bones.

bend

To create a lateral curve of the horse's body. The purpose is to allow the horse to make symmetrical turns with the hind feet to follow the tracks of the front feet. It is accomplished

Bell boots
(© MILLER HARNESS COMPANY L. L. C.)

Executing a bend
(© CHERRY HILL)

by the use of the rider's legs and hands; the horse is made to bend its body around the rider's inside leg (the leg closer to the center of the arena).

Bermuda grass
A grass used for hay.

between-the-legs shot
In polo, a stroke in which the player's mallet makes contact with the ball under the pony's belly.

bib martingale
A triangular piece of leather sewn between two forked chest straps. The device, which prevents horses from getting their feet caught in the tack, is most commonly seen during Thoroughbred racing exercise workouts.

bike
A light sulky used in Roadster Pony classes.

Bill Daly, on the
In racing, the tactic of taking a horse to the front at the start and then trying to remain on the lead all the way to the finish. The strategy capitalizes on a particular horse's running style of accelerating quickly and then maintaining that speed and stamina (as distinguished from horses with a come-from-behind ability). Named after trainer "Father Bill" Daly.

billet
One of the straps on a saddle to which the girth or cinch is buckled. All-purpose and competition saddles have three billet straps, of which two are used and the third is a spare. Dressage saddles have only two because an

extra strap would interfere with the contact between the rider's leg and the horse.

birdsfoot trefoil
A legume grass used for hay.

bishoping
Filing down a horse's teeth to give a false impression that the animal is younger than its real age. The word is said to come from the name of an unscrupulous eighteenth-century English horse dealer.

bit
The mouthpiece part of a bridle to which the reins are fastened. Bits control the horse's movement and direction by exerting pressure, sometimes in conjunction with other parts of the bridle, on the bars, cheeks, tongue, or roof of the mouth, the jaw, the nose, and the poll. Bits evolved from leather, bone, or bronze mouthpieces of antiquity into the modern era's sophisticated appliances made of metal (now usually stainless steel), rubber, or vulcanite. Bits can be categorized as either snaffle or curb and sometimes as a combination of the two *See also* on the bit, above the bit, behind the bit.

bit burr
A rubber disk with stiff burrlike projections on it. Inserted between the bit ring and the horse's cheek, the burrs press against the check when rein pressure causes the horse to turn, thus reinforcing the rein aid. Used primarily on racehorses.

bitch pack
In foxhunting, a pack of hounds that consists of only females. The advantage is that they

will not be distracted by the presence of male hounds (or vise versa).

bitting rig
A device comprised of a surcingle from which elastic side reins snap onto the rings of the horse's bit. Its purposes are to encourage a horse to accept a bit and to develop flexion at the poll.

black
A body color of true black, without any light areas; the mane and tail are also black.

Black Bess
The mare ridden by the notorious seventeenth-century British outlaw Dick Turpin.

blacksmith
A person who shoes horses; another word for *farrier*. The word comes from iron's having been considered a "black" metal (as distinguished from such "white" metals as tin).

black type
(1) In racing, bold-faced type used in sale catalogs to distinguish horses that have won or placed in a stakes race. If a horse's name appears in uppercase bold-faced type, it has won at least one stakes race. If the name appears in upper/lowercase bold-faced type, it has placed in at least one stakes race;
(2) A method of distinguishing successful show horses in horse show programs, sale catalogs, and so forth.

blaze
A broad, white vertical marking extending the length of the face, of a relatively uniform width narrower than a bald face.

bleeding
Rupturing of capillaries in the nose or throat that often causes choking. It is caused by excessive strain, most often occurring during a horse race. A horse with this condition is known as a bleeder and is treated with the diuretic furosemide (commonly called Lasix®).

blemish
Any permanent physical imperfection, such as a scar, that does not affect a horse's serviceability or soundness.

blinkers (also, blinders)
A pair of cups or flaps attached to the bridle or a hood, used to keep a horse from becoming distracted by seeing objects to the side or rear. They are routinely used in driving and harness racing and occasionally in flat racing.

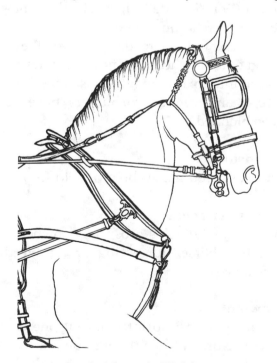

Carriage horse in blinkers
(© CHRISTINA BERUBE)

blister
To apply an irritant in order to draw blood to the area and relieve muscle or tendon strains. A once-prevalent practice, blistering has been replaced by such techniques as medication and acupuncture.

blister beetle
Often found in alfalfa, the blister beetle's body contains a highly toxic substance that can cause death if ingested; the poison first causes blisters in the horse's mouth and intestines. Prevention begins with examining bales of alfalfa for the insect's presence, then burning any such infected hay.

blood
(n) A term that describes the amount of Arabian or Thoroughbred in a horse's ancestry. A "blood" or "blooded" horse is all or mostly Arabian or Thoroughbred.
(v) In foxhunting, to dab a bit of the fox's blood onto the cheek of a novice hunter as initiation into foxhunting. Because kills are now rare, many veteran foxhunters have never been blooded.

bloodstock
Thoroughbred horses bred or sold for racing.

bloodstock agent
A person who helps prospective owners find and buy horses for racing or for breeding racehorses.

blow-out
In racing, a fast sprint workout one or two days before a race to sharpen a horse's speed.

blue
The color of the prize ribbon awarded for first place in the United States. (Curiously, red is the color of the first-prize ribbon in Great Britain and Ireland.)

bluegrass
A grass used as hay or roughage.

blue roan
A coat of white and black hairs, with black mane, legs, and tail.

blue stem
Any of several forage grasses grown in the Western United States.

board
Accommodations, feed, and care for a horse. *See also* full board, rough board.

bob
See nod.

bobble
To stumble, usually when leaving the starting gate in a race.

bobtail
A horse whose tail has been docked, or cut short, for decorative purposes or to keep mud off it. The term appears in Stephen Foster's "Camptown Races": "... bet my money on the bobtail nag/Somebody bet on the bay."

body brush
A grooming tool with relatively long, hard bristles, used to remove dirt and loose hair.

Body brush

bog spavin
A chronic swelling on the front of a hock due to a collection of fluid. Although the cause is not known, it most frequently occurs in horses with poor hind leg conformation. Since lameness does not occur, a bog spavin is often considered just an unsightly blemish. Treatments include draining the affected joint and administering anti-inflammatory medication.

bolt
To run away, usually out of control. Bolting usually results from an unexpected sight or sound that frightens the horse to the point of panic.

bone
A measurement taken around the leg below the knee or hock as an indication of a horse's projected ability to carry weight without injurious consequences. The phrase *good bone* refers to a large circumference.

bone spavin
A degenerative arthritis of the lower hock joint. Most often occurring in older horses, it is most prevalent in horses with poor hind leg conformation or those that have been subjected to hard work that puts stress on the hock (e.g., reining, polo, jumping, and harness racing). Treatment includes corrective shoeing, anti-inflammatory medication, and moderating the amount of work the horse does.

book
The group of mares bred to a stallion in a year.

bookmaker (or "bookie")
A person who accepts bets on horse races. The name comes from the practice of keeping a notebook in which wagers were entered. Bookmakers are licensed in Great Britain, Ireland, and other foreign countries, but are illegal in the United States.

boot hooks
Metal devices rounded at one end and with handles at the other, used to pull on tall boots.

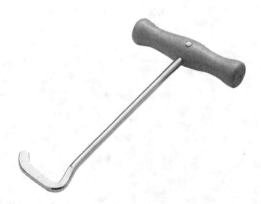

Boot hook
(© MILLER HARNESS COMPANY L. L. C.)

bootjack
A device into which the heel of a riding boot is inserted, to assist in removing the boot.

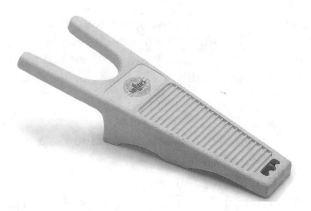
Bootjack
(© MILLER HARNESS COMPANY L. L. C.)

boot pulls
Fabric tabs on the inside of tall boots that help the wearer pull the boots on, with or without the use of boot hooks.

borium
A durable metal used as caulks in horseshoes, especially for riding in ice and snow.

bosal (bo-SAL)
A length of braided rawhide that is the part of a hackamore that applies pressure to a horse's nose and chin.

bots (or botflies)
The parasitic larvae of the *gasterophilus* fly. They appear as tiny yellow dots on a horse's lips and front legs and are ingested into the stomach, where they can cause colic and weight loss. A deworming program reduces the chance of a horse's being afflicted, as does shaving any eggs found on the horse's hair. Removing manure, in which the larvae and flies live, is another preventive treatment.

Bosal with rope fiador and mecate
(© CHERRY HILL)

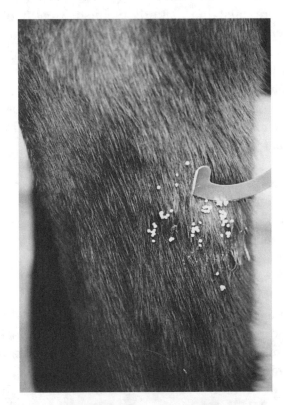
Botfly eggs on a horse's foreleg
(© RICHARD KLIMESH)

bottom
Endurance or stamina, most commonly used in describing a racehorse with staying power. The implication is that a horse with bottom has a great depth of stamina from which to draw.

bottom line
The maternal side of a horse's pedigree, so-called because the mare's lineage is listed on a chart below the sire's lineage

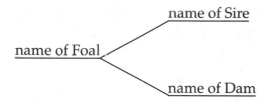

name of Sire

name of Foal

name of Dam

bounce
The familiar term for a combination of two fences set one cantering stride (usually twelve feet) apart. The horse will literally land over the first and immediately bounce over the second.

bowed tendon
An injury caused by the excessive stretching and tearing of a front leg's flexor tendon sheath. It is usually caused by repeated strain to the tendon, which then loosens from the cannon bone and develops the appearance of a taut archery bow. Initial treatment includes ice, support bandages, and anti-inflammatory medication, followed by prolonged rest until the bow "sets," or heals

Although a horse with a bowed tendon can return to work, the tendon will never regain its former strength.

bow hocks
A conformation fault in which the hocks are set too far apart and turn outward (the op-

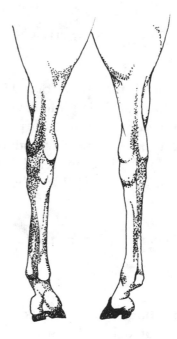

Bow hocks

(© CHRISTINA BERUBE)

posite of cow hocks). Also known as bow legs.

box
(1) A British term for horse van;
(2) In driving, the seat or platform on which the driver sits;
(3) In racing, a single bet that combines two or more horses to make multiple combinations. For example, an exacta box of horses identified by the numbers 1, 2, and 3 pays out if the order of finish is 1–2, 1–3, 2–1, 2–3, 3–1, or 3–2.

box stall
A square or rectangular compartment in which a horse lives. *See* straight stall.

bracer
Liniment used to rub down a horse after exercise.

23

bradoon
The snaffle bit of a double bridle.

braid
To twist a horse's mane and/or tail into single strands that are then tied into smaller pieces. Usually done for decorative purposes, braiding a mane also keeps the hair from flying into the rider's face. Braiding a tail keeps mud from collecting on it in foul weather.

bran
The husk of oats used in feed or in a mash as a laxative.

break
(1) To train a horse to accept tack and then accept a rider or driver. Because of the harsh methods that horsemen once used, such as encouraging a horse to buck and then trying to outlast him, the term now has an unpleasant connotation in this era of kinder and gentler methods. Accordingly, the word *start* is more frequently used in this connection;
(2) In racing, to leave the starting gate.

An illustration from a nineteenth-century book on horse training, showing a now-outdated breaking method

break down
To suffer an injury severe enough to end the horse's taking part in the race or other competition. In many instances, breaking down can end a horse's entire competitive career.

break off
To move a horse rapidly to one side by the use of the rider's lower leg or spur.

break stride
In harness racing, to go into a gallop instead of maintaining the trot or pace. If the driver does not immediately put the horse back on gait or if the break occurs at the end of the race, the horse will be disqualified.

breastcollar
A piece of tack that keeps a saddle from slipping back; also known as breastplate.

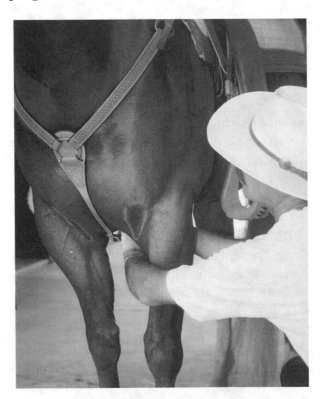

Western breastcollar

(© RICHARD KLIMESH)

breeches (BRIT-ches)
English riding pants having legs that extend to the calf. They are worn with tall boots. *Cf.* jodhpurs.

Breeches
(© MILLER HARNESS COMPANY L. L. C.)

breeching
In driving, wide harness bands that fit around the wheel horse's buttocks. The horse braces

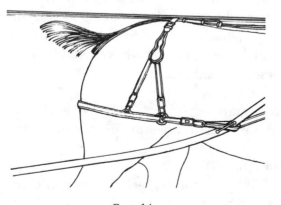

Breeching
(© CHRISTINA BERUBE)

back against the breeching assistance in slowing down or stopping the vehicle.

breed
(1) Any group of animals capable of passing along its distinctive characteristics. In the horse world, the word usually refers to any of more than one hundred recognized breeds that have been created and maintained by selective breeding by their owners and an organization's keeping a registry of pedigrees, such as the Jockey Club for Thoroughbreds or the Appaloosa Horse Club for that breed. In addition to "man-made" breeds are the ones that occur in nature, such as wild mustangs or the wild native ponies of Britain. Although these types of horses are not usually selectively bred, clubs and organizations exist for owners of horses of such breeds
(2) To mate a horse in order to produce a foal.

breeder
The owner of a dam at the time she is bred (according to the rules of the American Quarter Horse Association) or the owner at the time the dam gives birth (according to the rules of the Jockey Club).

Breeder's Cup
Thoroughbred racing's year-end championship, first run in 1984 and consisting of seven races conducted on one day at a different racetrack each year and for million-dollar purses. Winners in each category are widely considered that year's champion in that category: Juvenile (two-year-old colts at one mile); Juvenile Fillies; Spring (three-quarter mile); Mile; Distaff (fillies and mares at a mile and an eighth); Turf (a mile and a half); and Classic (a mile and a quarter). In addition, a

Breeder's Cup steeplechase race is held in conjunction with a hunt racing meeting somewhere along the eastern seaboard.

breeze
In racing, a fast short training gallop, usually timed, and often viewed as indicative of a horse's racing condition.

bridle
A headpiece consisting of a bit, straps to keep the bit in place, and a set of reins.

Bridle with snaffle bit

bridle hand
The rider's hand that holds the reins.

bridle path
(1) The clipped area of the mane running several inches behind the poll, where the crownpiece of the bridle lies. Its purpose is to keep the mane from becoming entangled in the bridle.
(2) A trail designed for horseback riding.

bridlewise
A relative and highly subjective view of a horse's responsiveness to directions from the reins and/or bit.

broken wind
Also known as heaves, a respiratory condition known as chronic obstructive pulmonary disease (COPD) marked by obstructions of airflow in the lungs. The symptom is difficulty in breathing and loss of energy. Causes include dust and allergies, especially when the horse is stabled in poorly ventilated quarters or on dusty bedding or is fed dusty hay. Most horses with COPD quickly respond to a change of environment away from whatever is causing the problem.

bromegrass (broom-grass)
A variety of hay grass.

bronc (or broncho)
Originally applied to an unbroken wild (in the sense of feral) horse, the term now refers to a bucking horse used in rodeo's saddle bronc and bareback bronc riding, two of the timed events in which the cowboy has to outlast the horse for eight seconds.

broodmare
A mare used for breeding purposes.

Brougham (BROOM)
In driving, a four-wheeled enclosed carriage with an exposed driver's box; named after a British nobleman.

browband
The part of the bridle that lies across the horse's forehead and holds the cheekpieces.

brown
(1) A body color of brown or black with light areas at the muzzle, eyes, flank, and inside upper legs; the mane and tail are black;
(2) The color of the prize ribbon awarded for eighth place.

brush
In foxhunting, the fox's tail. In the event of a kill, the brush is awarded as a trophy to a member of the hunt who was close to the hounds when they captured the fox.

brush boot
A piece of protective equipment worn on the fetlocks of horses that are prone to brushing.

brushing
Interference caused by one foot rubbing against or into the fetlock of the opposite foot.

Bucephalus
The favorite horse of Alexander the Great. As a young man, Alexander tamed the high-strung horse; noticing that the horse shied at its shadow on the ground, he faced the horse toward the sun and so calmed the animal. The name is Greek for "ox-headed."

buck
To jump with an arched back followed by landing on straightened legs.

buckaroo
A colloquial American term for cowboy, from the mispronunciation of the Mexican Spanish word *vaquero,* meaning cowboy.

bucked shin
An inflammation of the front of the cannon bone, usually of the front legs. Occurring in young horses, the condition happens when bones that cannot stand up to the stress of training fracture and hemorrhage. Treatment includes ice, rest, and in the case of severe fractures, surgery.

bucking strap
A snug leather strap placed around a rodeo bucking horse's flank to encourage him to buck; also known as flank strap.

buckskin
A dark-yellow or gold coat with a black mane, lower legs and tail, and no dorsal stripe.

bug boy
See apprentice.

bulb
One of the two wide areas on the back of the hoof.

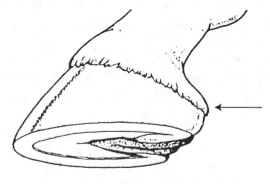

Bulb

bulldogging
The original term for steer wrestling. The word was suggested by the way a bulldog's teeth grip the face or the neck of a bull.

bump
(1) A Western term for a quick jerk of rein or a quick kick of leg pressure done variously to attract the horse's attention or to encourage it to shift its weight to its hind end;
(2) in jumping, a colloquial word for the schooling technique, usually done right before entering the showring, of intentionally riding a horse to a take-off spot that will cause its feet to strike the top rail of the fence. The purpose is to encourage the horse to try to be more careful and thus jump a rub-free round.

Burleigh (BURL-ee)
The major international horse trial held on the Marquess of Exeter's estate in Northamptonshire, England. Started in 1961, Burleigh ranks with Badminton, Lexington, and the Olympics as one of the world's most demanding three-day events.

bute
Phenylbutazone, a widely used nonsteroidal anti-inflammatory drug (NSAID) to reduce swelling and inflammation. Some racing commissions and horse show organizations restrict the amount permitted just prior to competition since it allows unsound horses to perform because they do not feel pain and thus are subjected to the possibility of further injury. Often known by the trade names Butazolidin and Butazone.

butt-bar
The restraining bar across the back of a trailer stall.

Buttermilk
The mare ridden by Dale Evans, "the Queen of the West," in the Roy Rogers cowboy movies and television series.

buy back
A horse that goes unsold through a public auction because it fails to reach its reserve bid.

buzkashi
An Afghanistani mounted game in which a sheep or goat carcass is carried across the goal line. The successful rider brings honor to himself as well as to his team (which is often his tribe or village).

by
A word indicating a horse's sire. "Secretariat was by Bold Ruler" means that Bold Ruler was Secretariat's sire.

Byerly Turk
Along with the Godolphin Barb and Darley Arab, one of the three Thoroughbred foundation sires, captured from the Turkish forces and imported to England in the mid-seventeenth century by Captain Byerly.

C

cadence
The rhythm of a horse's stride, often used to describe the regularity of steps.

Cadre Noir
The premier troupe of the French Cavalry School in Saumur, France. The name comes from the riders' black hats and tunics. Composed of twelve officers and twelve noncommissioned men, the Cadre Noir train and present their horses in haute école dressage and in jumping; riders take part in dressage, combined training, and show jumping competitions.

cala
A reining competition done by Mexican charros.

calf-kneed
A conformation fault in which the forelegs' carpal joints bend backward. It is considered a serious conformation fault since the knee will have a tendency to hyperextend backward. Also known as back at the knee.

calf roping
(1) A Western horse show class in which a horse is judged on how well it helps the rider

Calf roping

29

as the rider ropes a calf. In the best case scenario, the horse springs out of the starting box once the calf is released, maintains a position behind and to the side of the calf. Once the calf is roped, the horse slides to a stop, then backs up to maintain tension on the rope so the calf cannot evade the cowboy while he throws and hogties the calf's legs;

(2) In rodeo, an event in which the cowboy who ropes and ties three of the calf's legs in the fastest time is the winner.

caliente

A type of sturdy helmet worn predominantly by jockeys and combined training riders; named after Mexico's Agua Caliente Race Track where it was introduced.

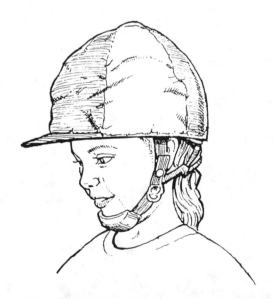

Caliente helmet

Camargue

A semiwild breed inhabiting the marshlands of southern France's Rhône River delta. Barely taller than a pony, with a compact body that is almost always gray in color, the Camar-

gue is the traditional mount of the region's cowboys called *gardians*.

cannon

The bone that extends from the knee or hock to the fetlock.

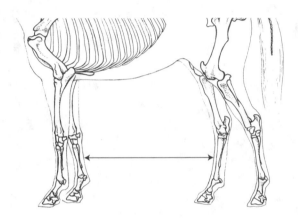

Cannon bones

(© CHRISTINA BERUBE)

canter

The horse's three-beat gait, a slow or collected gallop known in Western riding as the lope. The sequence of footfalls of a horse cantering

Horse cantering on its right lead

(© CHERRY HILL)

on its left lead is right hind, left hind and right fore simultaneously, and left fore. The name purportedly comes from the preferred gait of medieval pilgrims who traveled by horseback to the shrine of Thomas à Becket in Canterbury, England. *See* lead.

cantle
The elevated rear part of a saddle.

capillary refill time
The amount of time needed for blood to return to capillaries after it has been forced out of them (usually done by pressing the horse's gums). The return of the normal pink color indicates that the capillaries are refilled. The test measures certain aspects of the horse's general health.

capped hock
An infected swelling at the point of the hock.

capping fee
In foxhunting, the charge paid by nonmembers of the hunt for a day's sport; also called cap.

Caprilli, Federico [1868–1907]
Italian horseman credited with the development of the forward seat (which see).

capriole
The air above the ground in which the horse springs up out of a piaffe and kicks back with both hind legs while holding the forelegs close to its chest. The word comes from the Italian word for *goat*.

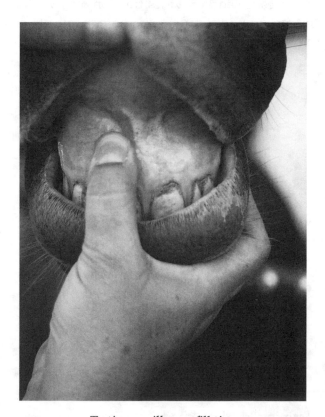

Testing capillary refill time

Lipizzaner performing a capriole

card
(1) The judge's scorecard;
(2) The day's or evening's program of racing.

carpus
The joint in the horse's front leg between the forearm and cannon, more commonly referred to as the knee.

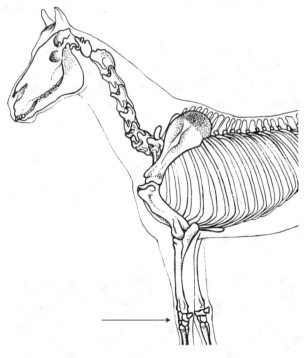

Carpus joints

(© CHRISTINA BERUBE)

carriage
(1) A vehicle designed to carry people in comfort and elegance;
(2) The style in which a horse carries itself, especially with regard to the head and neck position.

carrousel
An equestrian spectacle that was popular in eighteenth-century Europe and that featured mock battles and mounted ballets.

cart horse
Another term for a draft horse.

cast
A horse that is lying down on its side or back, wedged against the side of a stall in such a position that the animal cannot rise to its feet without assistance. As a verb, to throw a horse down onto the ground with the use of ropes or hobbles.

cathedral
A curb bit having a very high port.

caulk
A small stud that screws into a hole drilled into a horseshoe and provides traction over wet or frozen ground. Caulks are the equivalents of cleats or spikes on golf or baseball shoes.

A horseshoe with caulks

cavaletti
Training devices made of jump rails supported on low X-shaped holders or on blocks

32

Training a horse to jump using ground poles and cavaletti

and used primarily as jumping exercises. The name is Italian for "little horses" and, although plural, customarily refers to both one or more than one device.

cavalier
A mounted knight, an equestrian warrior. The word is now sometimes applied to male riders in a competition.

cavesson (CAV-uh-son)
The noseband of an English bridle.

Cavesson

cayuse (KIE-yoose)
Formerly a Native American horse descended from Spanish horses and now a familiar term for any Western horse. From the Cayuse tribe in present-day Oregon.

Centered Riding
A technique developed by the American instructor Sally Swift and published in 1985 in a book of the same name. Centered Riding emphasizes establishing and maintaining rider equilibrium as well as balance between horse and rider and involves visualization techniques, such as imagining that riders have eyes in their chest that turn to look in the direction they want their horses to turn.

chalk
In racing, the favorite horse among the bettors. The word comes from the former practice of writing odds in chalk on blackboards.

chambon (SHAM-bon)
A type of martingale that influences head and neck position by exerting pressure on the horse's poll.

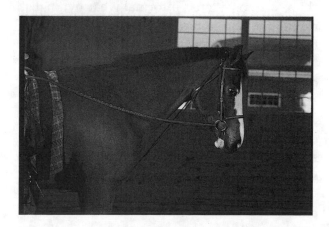

Chambon

(© MILLER HARNESS COMPANY, L. L. C.)

Champion
The sorrel horse ridden by the cowboy movie and television star Gene Autry.

change of lead
Going from one canter lead to the other. The transition can be either a simple change of lead or a flying change of lead. Known familiarly as swapping leads.

change of rein
A change of direction. To change to the right rein means to reverse the horse's movement from a counterclockwise to a clockwise direction. Also known as change of hand or change of school.

chaps
Leather leggings originally worn as protection against thorns, brush, and other sharp objects. Although that remains the reason why ranchers wear them, chaps (customarily pronounced "shaps" by Western riders and "chaps" by English riders), especially the snug-fitting "shotgun" variety, are now worn by both Western and English riders for leg support. Although chaps are considered informal wear by English riders, they are appropriate, if not mandatory, for certain Western horse show classes.

charger
A horse ridden by a cavalry officer.

charro
A horseman who rides in traditional Mexican equestrian events. *See* cala and colas.

check
In foxhunting, a pause by riders while the hounds search for a fox's scent.

check rein
In driving, a short strap that runs from the bit to the saddle of the harness to keep the horse from lowering his head.

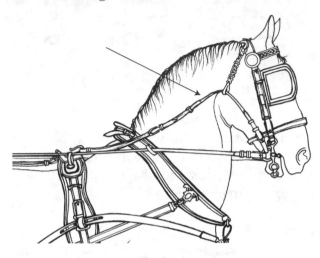

Check rein

(© CHRISTINA BERUBE)

cheek
The arm on some snaffle bits that prevents the rings of the bit from sliding out of the horse's mouth. A full cheek snaffle has arms above and below the ring; a half-cheek has arms only below the ring.

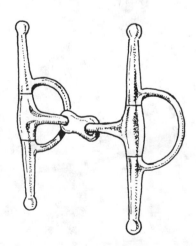

A full cheek snaffle (French mouth type)

cheekpiece
The strap on a bridle between the crownpiece and the bit. It rests against the horse's cheek and is adjustable so the bit can fit properly.

chestnut
(1) A dark red or brownish-red coat, mane, and tail. Although the term is often used synonymously with *sorrel*, chestnut is properly a slightly darker brown;
(2) One of the hard knoblike growths on the insides of a horse's legs (also called nighteye). Because chestnuts are as distinctive as human fingerprints, they are used as a mark of identification by breed registries and racing commissions.

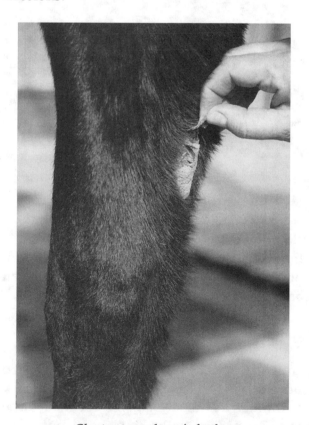

Chestnut on a horse's foreleg
(© RICHARD KLIMESH)

Chincoteague
A breed of feral ponies found on the islands of Chincoteague and Assateague off the coasts of Virginia and North Carolina. According to legend, they are descended from horses and ponies that washed ashore after shipwrecks in colonial times. Although most of the ponies live on Assateague, they are rounded up and swum across to Chincoteague every Memorial Day weekend where they are auctioned (the proceeds going to the local fire department). The breed received considerable exposure due to the popular children's book "Misty of Chincoteague" by Marguerite Henry.

chin groove
See curb groove.

chinks
Western chaps that cover the rider's legs above the knees. Worn with high boots that protect the rest of the leg, chinks enable cowboys to kneel while branding or otherwise tending to cattle.

chip
In jumping, an unwanted extra stride taken close to the fence before leaving the ground. Chipping produces an awkward jump for both horse and rider.

choker
A detachable turtleneck-style collar worn with women's ratcatcher shirts. The wearer's monogram stitched on the choker is a traditional touch.

chrome
A slang term for prominent white markings, such as stockings or socks.

chukkar
One of the periods into which a polo match is divided. Outdoor polo has eight chukkars lasting seven and a half minutes each. Arena (or indoor) polo has six chukkars of seven minutes in length. The word comes from the Hindu for "wheel," perhaps referring to the clock on which playing time was kept.

chute
(1) The pen from which calves used in calf-roping events are released;
(2) The extension to the backstretch or home stretch portions of some racetracks that permits a straight start instead of a start on a turn.

cigar
In polo, a type of mallet head in which both ends are tapered.

cinch
The strap on a Western saddle that passes under the horse's belly to hold the saddle in place. Some saddles, especially those used for roping, have two cinches for greater security.

circuit
(1) Several racetracks within a certain geographic area that have nonconflicting racing dates;
(2) A geographical division used with regard to certain horse show awards;
(3) A consecutive series of horse shows held at the same facility over a number of days.

claimer
In racing, a horse that is consistently run in claiming races.

Front cinch

(© RICHARD KLIMESH)

claiming price
In racing, the price for which a horse is running in a claiming race and for which he can be claimed.

claiming race
A race in which any horse so entered may be bought by a licensed owner at a stipulated price or within a range of prices either directly or through a trainer. Claims can be made until the race begins, with the claimed horse be-

coming the property of the new owner and the purse (if the horse wins one) going to the previous owner.

class
(1) An individual event within a horse show division;
(2) In racing, a horse showing the most impressive qualities of breeding and ability of all the horses in the race, as in the expression "the class of the race."

clean and fast
In three-day eventing, to incur no penalties in the speed-and-endurance phase. *Clean* refers to the absence of penalties for refusals or falls, while *fast* refers to the absence of penalties for exceeding the time limit.

clean-legged
A leg without a conformation fault or blemish.

clear round
In show or stadium jumping, a round in which the horse incurs no penalties for knockdowns, refusals, or exceeding the time allowed; also known as a clean round.

Cleveland Bay
The breed that originated in the Cleveland area of England's Yorkshire as a coach horse and agricultural worker. Infusions of Andalusian and other Spanish blood gave the horse a refined head and clean legs. As the name suggests, its color is bay with black points. Standing between sixteen and seventeen hands, the Cleveland Bay is often crossed with Thoroughbreds to produce an outstanding foxhunting horse.

clip
(1) To trim hair from a horse's body in any of several patterns (*see* hunter clip, trace clip);
(2) A metal projection on the toe of some horseshoes, the purpose of which is to help keep the shoe snugly in place.

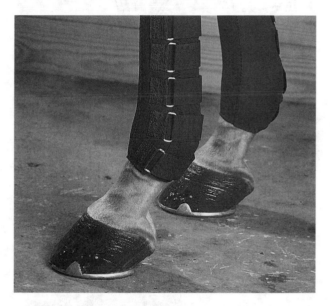

Toe clips
(© MILLER HARNESS COMPANY L. L. C.)

clocker
The racetrack official who times horses during their morning workouts.

close
To finish in a race. A horse that shows speed after being off the pace is called a quick closer.

close contact
A saddle with little or no padding in the seat and knee flaps. The phrase refers to the close contact between horse and rider, used in dressage and other disciplines that require subtle communication by the rider's seat and legs.

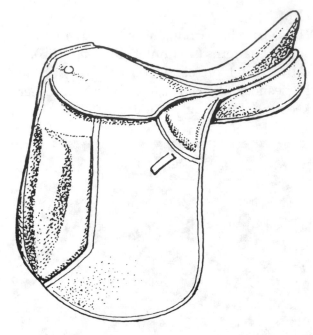

Close contact saddle for dressage

closing
In racing, the cutoff time after which nominations or entries are no longer accepted.

clover
A legume grass widely used for hay.

clubhouse turn
In racing, the turn of the track that comes after the finish line. It is so named because the preferred clubhouse seats face that part of the track.

Clydesdale
The draft breed that originated in eighteenth-century Scotland along the River Clyde. The breed was used for agricultural and industrial draft work, and by the mid-nineteenth cen-

Clydesdale

(© MAUREEN BLANEY)

tury became Scotland's most popular carriage horse. Standing from seventeen to eighteen hands high and weighing up to two thousand pounds, the Clydesdale is most typically bay or chestnut and has four white socks up to the knees and hocks, prominent feathers (silky hair on the back of its legs), and a high leg action at the walk and trot. Millions of people recognize the breed from their live and TV appearances pulling the Budweiser beer wagon.

coach horse
An individual or type of horse smaller than a draft horse yet strong enough to pull a driving vehicle.

coarse
See common.

cob
A type (not a breed) of riding horse distinguished by its good manners and ability as a saddle horse, especially its ability to carry heavy riders. Developed in Great Britain and Ireland, the cob has a thickset neck and body and short strong legs.

coffin
A cross-country obstacle composed of an open ditch with post-and-rail fences set in front and behind slopes on either side of the ditch.

coffin bone
The phalanx bone inside the foot; also known as the pedal (PEED-le) bone.

Coggins test
The test for equine infectious anemia devised by Dr. Leroy Coggins. A negative Coggins is routinely required for interstate shipping and for entering horses in competition.

colas
A Mexican charro event in which the rider grabs and twists the tail of a bull or steer, throwing it to the ground.

Colas competition
(© AMERICAN QUARTER HORSE ASSOCIATION)

cold blooded
A horse of all or mostly draft-horse breeding. The "cold blood" refers to the animal's characteristic calm manner. *See* hot blood; warm blood.

cold jawed
Unresponsive to bits.

cold shoeing
A farrier method of attaching preshaped shoes, as opposed to shoes that the farrier makes or fits by heating in the hot shoeing method.

colic
Any irritation, bloating, or blockage of the intestine, including a twisted intestine. Typical symptoms include sweating, lying down, nipping at the stomach, and otherwise trying to reduce or escape the pain, and a decrease in eating and in manure output. The seriousness of colic cannot be overemphasized; immediate veterinary attention is essential. Treatment may consist of doses of mineral oil (to help the horse pass the obstruction, if that is the prob-

lem) and intravenous fluids. In some instances, surgery to remove the obstruction or the section of twisted intestine may be required.

collar
In driving, the part of the harness that sits across the withers and shoulders and against which a horse pushes.

collect
To put a horse into a more compact frame, usually done to create greater impulsion (*Cf.* extend). Collection is most generally accomplished by the rider's legs and/or seat aids urging the horse forward while simultaneously the rider's hands restrain the amount of

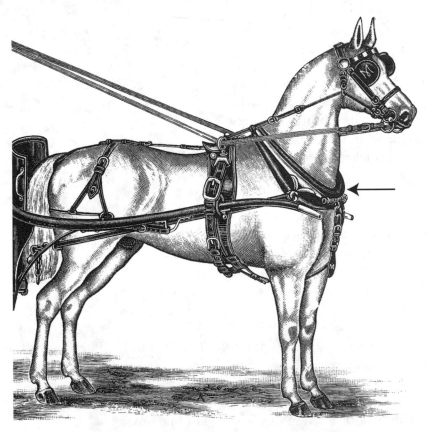

Collar

forward motion. The result is the horse's body being put into a "package."

colt
An ungelded male horse under four years old.

combination
In jumping, a series of two or three fences set apart at a total distance of forty feet. A horse that refuses the second or third element of a combination must go back and reattempt all two or three elements.

combined driving
A sport, similar to combined training, in which drivers and their horse or team of horses compete in three phases: dressage, hazards (also called cross-country or marathon), and obstacles (also known as cones).

combined training
The sport in which the same horse-and-rider combinations compete in dressage, speed-and-endurance (also called cross-country), and stadium jumping. Also known as eventing, such a competition is called a horse trial when it takes place over one or two days or a three-day event if that long (the dressage, cross-country, and stadium jumping will take place in that order on successive days). Combined training and eventing was known as the military because of the sport's cavalry origins; up until World War II, only cavalry officers took part in Olympic three-day eventing even though the sport had been one of the equestrian activities since 1912.

common
A pejorative term that indicates a lack of refinement or sharp definition in one or more particular features of a horse's overall conformation; a synonym is "coarse."

competitive trail ride
A competition in which the object is to finish an overland course of up to fifty miles as close as possible to the predetermined time. *Cf.* endurance (which is more of a race than a rally).

Concours Hippiques (con-COR ee-PEEK) French for "equestrian competitions," categories of national and international competitions conducted under Federation Equestre Internationale rules. They are designated as:

CN: Concours National, or National Competition, an intramural event within a country.

CA: Concors Amité, or Friendly Competition between two countries.

CI: Concours International, for more than two countries.

CSI: Concours International Officiel, with a Nations Cup (which see).

The above categories are further distinguished by the following letters at the end: S, for *saute* (jumping); D, for *dressage*; CC, for *concours complet* (eventing); and A, for *attalage* (driving).

condition book
A list published by the racing secretary of upcoming races, together with the criteria for entering a race and other relevant information.

conditions
The qualifications or eligibility rules for a particular race, such as the horse's age, sex, or the number of previous wins.

cones
See obstacles.

conformation
An individual horse's physical characteristics in relation to the ideal standards of the animal's breed or type or compared to any well-made horse. A conformation class in a horse show judges the entries on such standards.

contact
The degree of rein pressure against the horse's mouth. Also, the degree of closeness between the rider's seat and the saddle.

contracted heels
A condition where the foot narrows at the heels and causes lameness. The problem comes from faulty trimming or shoeing of the foot, and can be corrected with rest (during which time the foot heals) and proper shoeing.

cooler
A lightweight blanket or canvas sheet worn by the horse after exercise to prevent catching a chill.

coop
A jumping obstacle with two sloping sides and a flat top, resembling a chicken coop.

Corinthian
An obsolete term for an amateur sportsman. A Corinthian hunter class was an appointments class open only to members of recognized foxhunts.

corkscrew
A snaffle bit with a gently twisted mouthpiece.

Corkscrew bit
(© MILLER HARNESS COMPANY L. L. C.)

corn
A cereal plant whose kernels are used for feed.

corns
An injury that develops when shoes are left on the horse's feet for too long a time and cause pressure from the foot's growth being restricted by the shoe. Corns happen most commonly on the insides of the front feet. Proper foot care will clear up the problem.

coronet
The part of the foot to which the outer hoof wall is connected. Also known as the coronary band. *Cf.* hoof.

corral
A pen, usually round in shape, used to hold or to train horses.

corrective shoeing
A farrier technique to correct foot and leg problems or other conformation flaws by means of specially shaped shoes. Corrective shoeing can help such problems as toeing in and toeing out.

cottonseed meal
The crushed seed of the cotton plant, used as a laxative and a source of protein.

counter-canter
To canter intentionally on the incorrect lead, a balancing and suppling exercise for the horse. *See* wrong lead.

count strides
In jumping, to determine how many horse's strides will fit comfortably between two fences. Since four three-foot human strides equals one normal cantering stride, riders before a jumping event will walk the course on foot and measure off the distances in terms of their own strides.

couple
A pair of foxhounds. *Couple* is the unit by which hounds are counted, so seven hounds would be described as three-and-a-half couple. A young hound was often joined by a coupling leash to an older, better behaved hound, which gave rise to counting in terms of pairs.

coupled entry
Two or more racehorses owned or trained by the same person and running as a single wagering unit. Success by any horse in an entry will result in a payoff on that entry.

coupling
(1) The space between the last ribs and the loin; (2) A kind of leash that keeps two hounds side by side.

courbette
The air above the ground in which the horse rears and then performs a series of hops on his

Lipizzaner performing a courbette

(© TEMPLE FARMS)

hind legs. The word comes from the French for "crow."

courtesy circle
See opening circle.

cover
The act of live breeding, as distinguished from artificial insemination.

covert (COV-er)
In foxhunting, a thicket, den, or another likely place for hounds to find a fox.

cow
The colloquial term for a bovine other than a bull, whether it is a cow, heifer, steer, or calf.

cow-hocked
A conformation fault in which the hocks bow inward and the feet are widely separated.

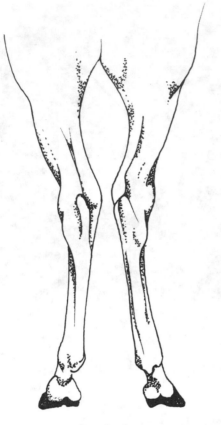

Cow-hocks

(© CHRISTINA BERUBE)

cowing
Of a cutting horse, completely focused on the cow that the horse is working.

cow kick
Of a bucking horse, to kick forward with the hind legs as a cow does.

cow pony
Any horse regardless of size that is used in ranch work.

cow sense
The innate (some say inherited) ability of a horse to work cattle as a cutting, roping, or

reining horse, most often found in American Quarter Horses and other Western breeds. A horse with this talent seems to anticipate the cattle's every move. Often shortened to "cow."

CPR
Shorthand for capillary refill test, pulse, and respiration, the three exams conducted during a vet check.

crack
A vertical split of the wall of the hoof, corrected by letting the foot grow out or by corrective shoeing

creep feeder
A feed apparatus with bars that are wide enough to allow a foal to eat grain but too narrow to let an adult horse reach in and take the foal's meal.

crest
The upper part of the neck from the withers to the poll.

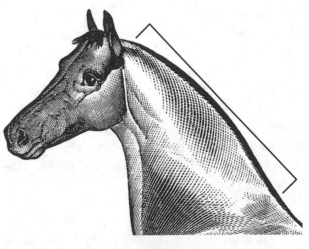

Crest

crest release

The hunter-seat equitation jumping technique in which the rider plants his hands on the horse's crest from takeoff to landing. The position supports the rider's upper body and keeps the hands from interfering with the horse's mouth. *Cf.* out-of-hand release.

cribbing

Sucking air into the lungs while biting onto a solid object such as a window ledge or feed bin. Often caused by boredom, this bad habit can be discouraged by a cribbing strap that is buckled snugly around the horse's neck and restricts the amount of air the horse can take in.

criollo

A breed found in Argentina, Brazil, and Peru that is descended from Spanish horses. Standing no taller than fifteen hands and dun in color, the criollo has a short head and muscular shoulders. It is used for ranch and pack work.

crop

(1) The group of foals sired by a stallion in a given season, or a group of foals owned by the same interest;
(2) A riding whip with a wrist loop at the handle end or the curved portion of a hunting whip.

cross-canter

A canter or lope where the horse's forelegs are on one lead and the hind legs are on the other lead. Allowing a horse to cross-canter is bad horsemanship. Also known as crossfiring or disunited canter.

crossing the line

In polo, a penalty in which a player crosses the imaginary line made by the flight of the ball. The reason for the rule is to prevent a collision when two or more players are in pursuit of the ball.

crossover

The act of forelegs or hind legs stepping over each other as the horse circles around his front or hind end, respectively. It is routinely seen in spins in reining classes and turns on the forehand or haunches in dressage and general schooling.

crossrail

A jump, usually low, that is composed of two rails that meet to form an X. Crossrails, which can be easily trotted as well as cantered, are most often used for training young horses and novice riders.

Crossrail

cross tie

To secure a horse by two ropes, each of which extends from a wall to one side of the animal's halter. A horse that is crosstied has its movement restricted and is thus easier to groom or otherwise handle.

croup
The rump from loin to dock. *Cf.* loin.

croupade
An air above the ground in which the horse leaps off the ground and keeps his hind legs close to his body; a variation of the capriole. *Cf.* ballotade.

crow-hop
To buck forward in a straight line.

crownpiece
The part of a bridle that fits behind the horse's ears.

crupper
A leather strap that goes under the horse's tail and keeps the harness or saddle from slipping forward.

cryptorchid (cryp-TOR-kid)
A male horse with one or both undescended testicles; also known as a ridgeling.

cubbing
The early part of the foxhunting season during which young hounds are introduced into the pack. Cubbing usually begins in late summer and lasts until the beginning of the formal season, which generally starts in October. Riders wear far more informal clothing while cubbing than they do during the formal season. The name comes from efforts to induce fox cubs to leave their parents' den and establish residences of their own (so there will be a wider distribution of quarry around the countryside).

cue
The primarily Western term for a signal from the rider to the horse. *See* aid.

cuppy
In racing, a loose and dry track surface on which horses have difficulty getting good footing.

curb
(1) A hard swelling or thickening of the ligament that runs along the hock. It is caused by strain and may or may not cause lameness; it may remain after the animal is rested;
(2) One of the two main categories of bits (the other is snaffle). A curb bit's port and shanks create a lever effect on the bars and roof of the horse's mouth to which the animal reacts by arching its neck and/or stopping. The height and width of the port and the length of the shanks determine the mildness or severity of

Curb bit with chain

the bit. Curbs are traditionally worn by Western horses.

curb chain (or strap)

A chain (or strap) worn with a curb bit under the horse's jaw to increase the bit's leverage effect.

curb groove

The groove in the back of the horse's jaw.

curry

To clean a horse with a curry comb. Also, a general term for cleaning a horse's body, mane, and tail.

curry comb

A grooming tool with stubby hard rubber bristles, used in a circular motion to remove caked dirt.

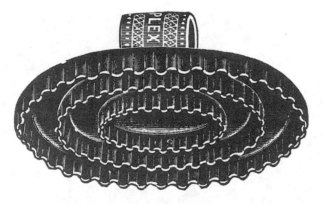

Curry comb

cut

(1) To separate a cow or calf from a herd;
(2) Colloquially, to geld a male horse.

cutter

(1) The rider in a cutting horse event;
(2) The driver in cutter and chariot racing.

cutting

A Western horse show class or separate event in which a horse separates (or cuts) a cow from the herd and then prevents it from returning to the herd. Once the rider indicates to the horse which cow is to be worked, the rider is not permitted to guide the horse. The horse stays between the cow and the herd, blocking the cow's efforts to get back to the herd by moving its body in almost a mirror image to the cow's. The cut ends when either the cow manages to slip past the horse or it is evident that the cow cannot return to the others. Horses, which have two minutes to perform, are judged on their agility and success, with the degree of difficulty of the cow also taken into account. Since certain strains of American Quarter Horses and other Western breeds excel at cutting, the ability is thought to be inherited. *See* alligator; cowing; leak; peel; shape; sour; and turnback.

A cutting horse at work

(© D.R. STOECKLEIN/AMERICAN QUARTER HORSE ASSOCIATION)

daisy cutter
An expression for a horse that has a long, low stride.

Dales
A breed of pony native to the north of England. It was developed in the eighteenth and nineteenth centuries as a pack pony. Its strong shoulders and legs make the Dales pony good for riding and driving.

dally
To wrap a lariat rope around the saddle horn after a steer or calf has been roped. The word comes from the Spanish phrase *de la vuelta*, to make a turn (of the rope).

dally team roping
A Western horse show event in which the horse is judged on its ability to maintain its position relative to the calf as the mount of

Dally team roping
(© WYATT MCSPADDEN/AMERICAN QUARTER HORSE ASSOCIATION)

either the header or the heeler in team roping. In the rodeo event called team roping, the fastest time for a pair of riders to rope a steer's head and hind legs determines the winner.

dam
A horse's female parent, or a broodmare.

dangerous riding
In polo, a foul committed by a player who rides in a manner that puts other players at risk; for example, by zigzagging up or down the field.

dapple gray
A light gray body covered with rings of a darker gray. The rings themselves are called dapples.

Darley Arab
Along with the Byerly Turk and Godolphin Barb, one of the three Thoroughbred foundation sires. Foaled around 1702 and imported to England from the Middle East by a Mr. Darley, the horse was the most important sire of the three in terms of the number of successful racers who sprang from his line.

Dartmoor
A breed of pony native to the Dartmoor Forest in the west of England. Like other native

Dartmoor mare and foal
(© CYNTHIA BRANN)

British breeds, it stands between twelve and thirteen hands high. The Dartmoor has a long, low comfortable stride, and because of its Arabian and Thoroughbred blood, is one of the more refined of the native pony breeds.

daylight
In calf roping, to allow the calf to get up before throwing it down and beginning the tie. A calf that was jerked down by the thrown rope and remains on the ground when the roper reaches it must be daylighted.

dead heat
In racing, two or more horses crossing the finish line simultaneously or too close to tell which one finished ahead of the other or others (there have been examples of triple dead heats). All horses involved in a dead heat are considered as tied for that position.

dead weight
In racing, the difference between the amount of weight the horse is assigned to carry and the weight of the jockey. Any difference will be carried as lead bars in the saddle pad, hence the term *dead weight* (as opposed to the rider's live weight).

declaration
Withdrawing an entered horse from a race before the closing of overnight entries. *See also* scratch.

deep
In jumping, a take-off point that is too close to the jump, making the jumping effort awkward for the horse and uncomfortable for the rider. Another term is *tight*. The opposite is *long*.

defended penalty shot
In polo, a penalty shot which the opposing team may try to block. *See* undefended penalty shot.

dental star
The darker dentin that fills a tooth's pulp cavity as the tooth wears down.

derby (DUR-bee in America; DAR-bee in Britain)
(1) A hat with a rounded crown and small brim, worn on formal occasions by some fox hunters, dressage riders, and gaited horse riders;
(2) *Capitalized*, any of the classic races for three-year-old Thoroughbreds such as the Kentucky Derby and the Epsom Derby. Like the hat, the race was named for the twelfth Earl of Derby, who owned a horse that won the first English Derby.

destrier
A warhorse. The word comes from the Latin for "right," which was the side on which a knight's squire would lead the horse.

dewormer (dee-WORMER)
Oral medication that rids the horse of parasites. The word is used interchangeably with *wormer*.

diagonal
The rider's posting motion in relation to the horse's trotting steps. A rider who rises when the horse's left foreleg and right hind leg strike the ground when the horse is moving counterclockwise is posting on the left diagonal. The theory is to keep the rider's weight off the outside hind leg when the horse is moving in a circle because that leg provides more of the impulsion.

direct rein
Rein pressure created by the rider's hand being drawn back toward the hip on that side of the horse. The direct rein is the primary way to control speed and direction. *See* indirect rein; neck rein; opening rein.

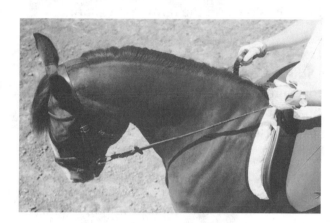

Turning left using direct rein
(© RICHARD KLIMESH)

dish faced
Having a concave face, typical of Arabian horses.

distaff
A racing term for fillies and mares. A distaff was a spindle used in weaving, considered a task for females.

distance
In jumping, the place from which the horse leaves the ground in relation to the fence's location. Seeing a distance refers to the rider's sensing, in terms of number of strides, where the horse is in relation to the fence. Experienced riders can then shorten or lengthen the horse's stride, if need be, in order to arrive at an optimum take-off point. *See* deep; long.

disunited
See cross-canter.

division
Any of the major horse show categories. Examples are the hunter division, the conformation division, and the reining division.

DMSO
Dimethyl sulfoxide, a topical anti-inflammatory agent that is used to administer medication by being absorbed into the horse's system through the skin.

dock
The fleshy root of the tail. As a verb, to cut the tail at or above the dock, originally done to carriage horses so their tails would not become entangled in the harness or blow into the driver's face.

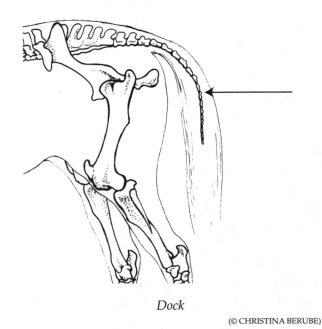

Dock

(© CHRISTINA BERUBE)

Doctor Bristol
A variety of snaffle bit with a mouthpiece that has three joints. The midsection produces pressure on the horse's tongue while the other two pieces work against the horse's cheeks.

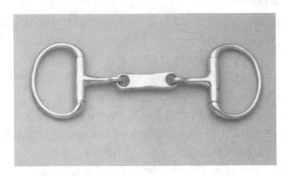

Doctor Bristol bit
(© MILLER HARNESS COMPANY L. L. C.)

dog
(1) In foxhunting, a member of any breed other than foxhound; or a male hound;
(2) In racing, one of the rubber cones placed out from the track's rail during training sessions in wet weather to prevent hooves from digging up the inside part of the racing strip.

donkey
Another name for domestic ass.

dorsal
Of or pertaining to the spine.

double bridle
An English bridle containing both a snaffle and a curb bit. It is designed to hold two separate bits in the horse's mouth. The bridle has two headpieces that pass through the loops of the browband and attach to two separate sets of cheekpieces. One cheek holds the bradoon bit while the other cheek holds the curb bit

Fitting a double bridle

(Weymouth), which lies in the mouth directly below the bradoon. The actions of the bradoon and the Weymouth are controlled through separate sets of reins, permitting the rider a large reining vocabulary for communicating with the horse. Also known as a full bridle or Weymouth.

double clear
(1) In a two-round show jumping competition, incurring no faults in both rounds;
(2) In competitive driving, no time or knockdown penalties in the cones phase.

double-jointed snaffle
A snaffle bit whose mouthpiece has two joints instead of the customary one.

double rigged
Of a Western saddle, having two cinches.

down
The direction toward the ring's or arena's gate. To jump down a line (of fences) is to start

with the fence farthest away from the gate and head toward the jump closest to the gate. *See* up.

draft breeds
Any of the breeds of large horses used for heavy pulling, such as the Percheron, Clydesdale, and Shire. Descendants of the Flemish Great Horse, all were developed in regions that had abundant and nutritious pasturage that enhanced growth and size. Also known as cold bloods.

drag
(1) To bring up the rear of a herd of cattle while moving or driving them;
(2) To smooth the surface of an arena before or between rounds of a competition;
(3) In driving, a four-wheeled coach with seats on top of and inside the vehicle.

drag hunt
A fox hunt in which the hounds follow an artificial scent that is laid down across the countryside before the hunt begins.

draw
The horse's position in a horse show event's starting order or a horse race's post positions. For example, "the favorite drew the eighth post position." The word comes from the positions being randomly chosen by drawing numbers out of a box.

draw reins
A training device consisting of a pair of reins that passes from the horse's girth between the forelegs and through the bridle rings back to the rider's hands. Draw reins are used to encourage a horse to flex its head and neck.

drench
To give (a horse) liquid medication.

dressage (druh-SAHZE)
Schooling a horse accordingly to principles based on progressive stages (the idea is that each stage leads out of the preceding stage). The word comes from the French for "training." As a competition, horses and riders perform a test of stipulated sequences of movements and transitions. Levels of tests range from elementary patterns of walking, trotting, and centering to the most advanced tests that include piaffe, passage, and flying changes of lead. Each movement and transition is scored from zero (not performed) to ten (perfect). The total, plus additional points for regularity of gait, impulsion, rider position, and other factors, determines the entry's score.

Dressage

dressage whip
A long thin whip approximately thirty to thirty-six inches. Its length permits the rider

to use it to reinforce leg aids without having to remove the whip hand from the rein.

dress boots
Knee-high, plain-front boots worn in English riding. *Cf.* field boots.

D ring
(1) A snaffle bit that has rings shaped like the letter D. The purpose is to restrict the amount the rings can turn, which would diminish some of the effect of the reins;
(2) The D shaped rings on a saddle to which a breastcollar or latigo is laced or buckled.

driver
In harness racing, the person in the sulky.

driving
(1) Of a horse, pulling a cart or another vehicle;
(2) A method of controlling a horse by means of long reins held by a person who walks behind the horse; the technique is used to train a young horse that has not yet been ridden or a horse that will pull a vehicle;
(3) In racing, winning with effort.

Driving a young horse

driving aids
The combination of a rider's seat and legs that encourages a horse to move forward.

dropdown
In racing, a horse that is facing a lower class of competition than encountered in its previous race.

drop fence
A cross-country obstacle, the landing side of which is lower than the take-off side.

Drop fence

dropped noseband
An attachment that buckles onto the front of a cavesson and fastens around the horse's jaw to keep the animal's mouth closed so the bit can have greater effect. Also known as a hinged noseband or a hinged dropped cavesson.

dry work
The opening reining phase in a working cow horse class. The dry work is followed by the fence work.

duck
Of a jumping rider, the error of dropping the head and upper body on one side of the horse's neck while in the air. Besides looking awkward, this sudden movement disturbs the horse's balance and may lead to the animal's hitting the fence.

dun
Yellowish or gold body with black or brown legs and tail, a dark dorsal stripe running the length of the spine, and often stripes on the legs and over the withers.

Dutch warmblood
A breed native to the Netherlands, originated by crossing Thoroughbreds and European warmblood types with native horses. Strong and athletic, Dutch Warmbloods are used as dressage and show jumping horses.

dwell
Of a jumping horse, to give the impression of hanging in the air over a fence, usually due to a lack of impulsion or hesitancy about leaving the ground or landing.

early foot
In racing, showing speed in the early stages of a race.

ease
In racing, to pull up a horse gradually, either because the jockey thinks the horse has no chance to improve its position or because the animal has an injury.

Eastern Equine Encephalomyelitis (EEE)
A very contagious and usually fatal viral infection that affects the horse's brain and spinal cord. Spread by mosquitoes, EEE can be prevented by annual vaccinations.

Eclipse Awards
Year-end honors given to outstanding horses, jockeys, and others involved in Thoroughbred racing. The award is named after the legendary eighteenth-century English racehorse.

eggbutt snaffle
A snaffle bit with oval rings. The shape of the rings holds the reins in a more direct line with the rider's hands (as opposed to round rings, which let the reins slide around on them more easily).

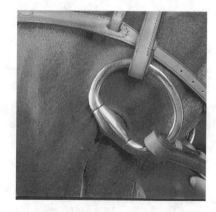

Eggbutt snaffle
(© MILLER HARNESS COMPANY L. L. C.)

elbow
The joint connecting the foreleg to the body.

element
In jumping, one of the components of an obstacle or combination, such as the top rail of a fence or the second jump in a double combination.

elevator bit
A variety of snaffle bit with a series of rings or a long bar on the sides. The reins can be attached to any of the rings, so the bit offers options: the lower the reins are attached, the greater the degree of leverage the elevator works to produce increased flexion and control.

Elevator bit
(© MILLER HARNESS COMPANY L. L. C.)

elimination
The involuntary end of competition for an entry that has exceeded a certain standard, such as, in show jumping, incurring more than two refusals or going off course.

embryo transplant (or transfer)
The reproduction procedure in which an embryo is removed from its mother and im-

planted into the womb of a second (the so-called carrier) mare. The purpose is to allow the original mother to be bred again.

endurance
A type of long-distance competition in which riders try to finish the course as quickly as possible (as distinguished from a competitive trail ride). *See also* speed and endurance.

engagement
The action of the horse's hind legs that propel the animal with impulsion; also known as engagement of the hocks.

English
Referring to any of the riding styles that involve a flat, hornless saddle, as distinguished from Western riding. Also, the equipment used in this style. Although the techniques are European in origin and not just British, the name came from the style's association with the predominant style along the eastern seaboard, especially with regard to foxhunting tack. That is why the style is sometimes referred to as eastern riding.

enter
To enroll a horse in a race, horse show, rodeo, or other competition.

entire
A male horse that has not been gelded; a stallion.

entry
In racing, two or more horses in the same race that have common ties of ownership, leasing, or training. *See* coupled entry.

entry fee
Money paid to enroll a horse in a competition.

eohippus
The earliest true equine, appearing during the Eocene era 55 million years ago. The size of a small dog, eohippus had four toes on each forefoot and three toes on the back feet (the toes evolved into a single hoof). The word is Latin for "dawn horse."

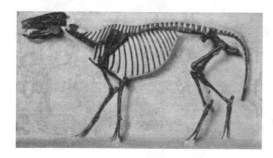

Skeleton of eohippus

Equine Infectious Anemia (EIA)
A circulatory disease, also known as swamp fever, caused by bacteria and producing a decrease in red blood cells that weakens a horse with the disease. There is no known treatment or cure for EIA, which is detected by the Coggins Test.

equitation
Another word for horsemanship.

equitation over fences
A horse show class in which riders are judged on their form and control over a course of jumps.

ergot
A harmless thick callus growth composed of hair masses at the back of the fetlock joint.

ermine marks
Small black markings that often appear on the coronet band.

estrus
The period during which a mare is sexually receptive; at that time the mare is said to be "in season" or "in heat." The estrus cycle relates to the amount of daylight, increasing during spring and summer months and decreasing during autumn and winter. The length of the cycle averages three weeks, with estrus lasting approximately one week.

even money
In racing, odds at which successful bettors receive back as much as they have wagered. Even-money odds are indicated as 1 : 1 and indicates the betting favorite.

eventing
The popular term for combined training or three-day eventing.

ewe necked
A conformation fault in which the neck is wider at its top than at its bottom.

exacta
In racing, a type of wager in which the horses that finish first and second must be selected in that order; also known as perfecta.

exercise rider
In racing, a person who is licensed to gallop horses during morning workout training sessions.

Exmoor
A breed of pony native to the Exmoor moorlands in the west of England. The oldest of the native British pony breeds, the hardy Exmoor measures only some twelve hands high, but is strong enough to carry an adult rider.

extend
To increase the length of the horse's stride, accomplished by the rider's increasing the driving aids and relaxing rein pressure. *Cf.* collect; *see* move up.

Falabella
See Miniature Horse.

farrier
A person who shoes horses; also known as horse shoer or blacksmith; from *fer*, the French word for "iron."

fast
In racing, a track surface that is dry and even; the optimum condition for a dirt tack (the turf equivalent is *firm*).

fault
(1) The unit of penalties in jumper classes for knocking down or refusing to jump an obstacle or for exceeding the time limit;
(2) A flaw or blemish in a horse's conformation. Conformation faults occur in degrees: some can be so severe they affect the animal's way of going, while other less severe faults are simply cosmetically unattractive.

feather
In foxhunting, of a hound, to wag its tail in excitement at the sight or scent of a fox. The word presumably comes from the image of a waving plume.

feathers
The long hairs on the fetlocks of certain draft breeds.

Fedération Équestre Internationale (F.E.I.)
The international governing body of horse sports, located in Berne, Switzerland.

feed bag
A fabric container that holds grain or pellets. It fits over the horse's muzzle and is used for feeding when the horse is not in his stall.

F.E.I.
See Fedération Équestre Internationale.

Fell
A breed of pony native to the northwest of England. Influenced by the Friesian horse, this sturdy, predominantly black pony stands approximately fourteen hands high and is equally adept at being ridden or driven.

fence work
The second phase of the working cow horse class, in which the horse maneuvers the cow down the long side of the arena, then into the center where the cow is made to turn in both directions. The horse must be able to work close to the cow to influence the cow's movements and not let the cow escape. *See also* dry work.

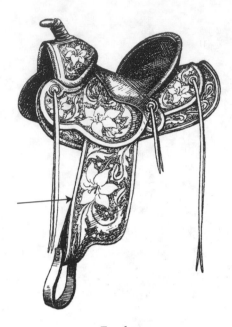

Fender

fetlock
The joint between the pastern and the cannon bones.

Turning a cow during fence work
(© WYATT MCSPADDEN/AMERICAN QUARTER HORSE ASSOCIATION)

fender
The wide panel between the seat and stirrup of a Western saddle. It protects the rider's leg from rubbing against the horse's side.

fescue
A variety of hay grass.

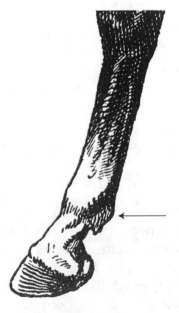

Fetlock

fiador (FEE-a-dor; sometimes THEE-a-dore) The part of some hackamores that goes over the horse's poll and knots behind the jaw to keep the bosal in place.

The fiador is the white rope visible behind the bosal
(© CHERRY HILL)

field
In foxhunting, the collective term for riders (other than the hunt staff) who follow the hounds.

field boots
Knee-high boots with laced feet.

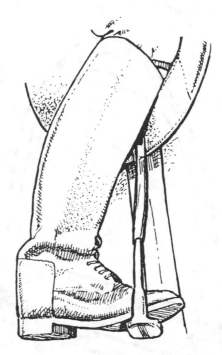

Field boot

field master
In foxhunting, the member of the hunt staff who is responsible for leading the field, especially with regard to keeping them from riding too close to and interfering with the hounds.

figure eight
A type of noseband made of two pieces that cross over the horse's nose and buckle behind the bit rings. It is especially effective in keep-

ing the horse's mouth closed and thus increasing the bit's influence.

Fillis stirrup
An English-style stirrup with slightly rounded sides. The most widely used style today, it was invented by James Fillis (1834–1913), English trainer and author.

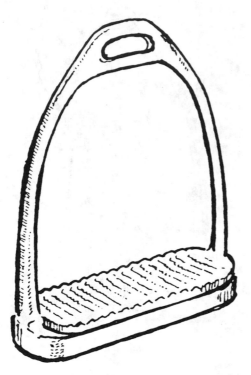

Fillis stirrup

filly
A female horse under the age of four and that has not had a foal (if she has had one, the horse is called a mare, no matter what her age).

Fine Harness
A horse show division for three-gaited Saddlebreds that pull a light four-wheeled vehi-

cle. The horse is judged on its action, elegance, and manners.

finishing brush
A grooming tool with relatively soft bristles, used to put a final sheen on the horse's coat.

firm
In racing, a turf surface having solid, compact footing; the turf equivalent of a dirt track's *fast*.

first-year green
A show hunter that is in its first year of showing in the hunter division. Fences in these classes are set at three feet three inches.

fistulous withers
A deep infection at the withers coming from a break in the skin that has become contaminated with bacteria. Treatment involves cleaning the wound so it can heal properly and treating the infection with antibiotics.

fit
In excellent physical condition.

five-gaited
Of American Saddlebreds, able to move at the walk, trot, canter, slow gait, and rack. *Cf.* three-gaited.

fixture card
In foxhunting, the list of locations where hunts will start out throughout the season. Fixture cards are distributed at the beginning of the hunting year.

Fjord pony
A breed of pony native to Norway. Invariably dun in color with its mane trimmed to stand

upright, the fjord pony is noted for its compact shape and rugged constitution. It is used for both riding and driving.

flake
A section of baled hay usually measuring from eight to twelve inches wide.

flak jacket
The familiar term for the protective safety vest worn by jockeys, combined training riders during the cross-country phase, and many other riders.

Flank

flap
The panel on an English saddle that covers the billets and protects the rider's leg from being rubbed by them.

flash cavesson
A noseband with diagonally crossed straps attached to the top of the noseband that fasten

Flak jacket

flank
The part of the body between the ribs and the hip.

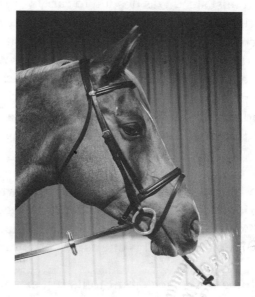

Flash cavesson

(© CHERRY HILL)

around the back of the horse's jaw. The straps keeps the horse's mouth closed so the bit can have great effect, while the noseband permits the use of a standing martingale.

flat
In English-style riding, riding in an arena without jumping, as in the expression "working on the flat." Also, as a verb, to exercise a horse without jumping.

flat racing
A term used to distinguish racing that is not harness (Standardbred racing) or over fences (steeplechase or hunt racing).

flea-bitten gray
A gray coat with tiny dark flecks or spots.

Flemish Great Horse
The medieval mount of knights in armor, originating in present-day Belgium. When a large and robust steed was needed to carry warriors wearing up to one hundred pounds of armor, selective breeding of the biggest animals to be found produced the Flemish Great (or War) Horse. Many were exported to other parts of Europe. When the age of chivalry ended, descendants of these warhorses were used to breed draft horses to pull plows and wagons.

flex
(1) A dressage or training technique in which the rider causes the horse to bend its head at the poll while simultaneously the animal's jaw accepts the bit. It is one aspect of putting a horse on the bit;
(2) To bend the hock joint to its full extent, as in the veterinary hock flexion test to determine lameness.

float
To file down the sharp edges of a tooth to keep the edges from cutting into the inside of the horse's mouth. A rasp file is used for this procedure.

Floating a horse's teeth

flocking
The padding material of the panels of a saddle. The material can be wool, a wool-synthetic blend, cotton, foam rubber, or felt.

flying change of lead
A switch of leads at the canter or lope without breaking stride to the trot or walk. It is accomplished (on a horse that has been so trained) by the rider's shifting his weight to ask the horse to shift its weight, then applying the canter aids for the other lead. *Cf.* simple change of lead.

Flying change of lead

fly sheet
A light, sometimes mesh blanket worn in warm weather to shield against insects.

fly whisk
A whiplike device having a clump of horse-hair at one end, used to brush away insects during a ride.

foal
A colt or filly under the age of one year (*see* suckling; weanling); as a verb, to give birth to a horse.

footing
The condition of an arena or racetrack. Also known as *going,* as in the expression "hard going."

fore
Short for foreleg or fore foot.

forearm
The portion of the foreleg between the elbow and the knee.

forehand
The part of the horse in front of the barrel. *See also* heavy on the forehand.

forelock
The portion of the mane between the ears and over the forehead.

forging
An interference in which the hind feet strike the backs of the forelegs or feet; also known as overreaching.

form
In racing, an evaluation of a horse's ability, based on breeding, past performance, and current workouts. A horse that is considered competitively fit is said to be "in good form."

formal season
The part of the foxhunting year from the end of the cubbing season to the end of the hunting year (usually when winter weather makes hunting difficult to impossible or, in warmer climates, the beginning of spring when foxes give birth to their cubs).

forward seat
In English riding, the position for jumping in which the rider inclines his or her upper body

Forward seat

at the waist so it can be held over the horse's center of gravity (which is above or ahead of the withers during a jump). Also, a close-contact saddle designed to facilitate this position.

foul
In racing, an action by a horse or jockey, such as cutting off another horse. If the patrol judge and/or the stewards feel that the action affected or might have affected the outcome of the race, the offending horse will be disqualified and the order of finish changed accordingly.

foundation sire
A stallion to whom the lineage of all members of a breed can be traced back. Foundation sires include Janus for American Quarter Horses, Justin Morgan (also known as Figure) for Morgans and, for Thoroughbreds, the Byerly Turk, Godolphin Barb, and Darley Arabian.

founder
Chronic laminitis.

four-in-hand
In driving, a vehicle pulled by four horses, two leaders in front and two wheelers behind them.

foxhound
The breed of dog used in the sport of foxhunting. There are two strains, the American and the English, with the latter somewhat smaller in size.

fox hunting
The pursuit of foxes by hounds, which are in turn followed by riders. Foxhunting arose in eighteenth-century Britain when Parliament

A four-in-hand park drag

ordered that fields be enclosed. Wood and brush fencing and earthwork banks and ditches proved to be appealing jumping obstacles for riders who began to follow hounds that hunted foxes as a method of predator control (foxhunting is also known as riding to hounds). British colonists introduced the sport to America; Washington and Jefferson were avid hunters. Centuries-old traditions of dress are scrupulously observed, such as the scarlet (called pink) coats worn by members of the hunt staff. More than 150 hunts in North America include drag hunts that pursue artificial scent instead of live quarry.

fox trot
A gait in which the back feet trot while the front feet walk. Most widely seen done by the Missouri Fox Trotter breed, the gait provides a smooth and comfortable ride.

frame
The outline or overall shape of a horse. "In a frame" or a "round frame" refers to a horse whose hind legs are stepping up under its

body to generate impulsion (as opposed to being strung out behind) and whose neck is flexed. "In a frame" is something of a synonym for "on the bit."

free rein
An extension of the reins to almost their full length, to allow the horse to lower and extend its neck as a relief from work at a more controlled position. Many dressage tests end with the horse leaving the arena on a free rein.

freestyle
An upper-level dressage test in which the riders design their own sequences of movements and transitions; they are judged on both their horses' performances and the creativity of their tests.

French mouth
A type of snaffle bit, similar in construction to the Doctor Bristol (which see), but with a figure-eight shaped midsection.

fresh
(1) Of cattle, not been previously used for cutting or team penning;
(2) Frisky.

Friesian
A breed characterized by its black coat, fetlock feathers, and long full mane and tail. Related to the Flemish Great Horse, the breed has influenced the Shire, Oldenburg, and several of the British native ponies. The Friesian, whose name comes from the Freisland region of the Netherlands, is used for driving and, to a lesser degree, riding.

frog
The soft V-shaped portion of the sole of the foot. *Cf.* hoof.

front-runner
In racing, a horse that runs on or near the lead at the start and then tries to hold or improve that position.

full board
A stabling arrangement whereby the fee for the boarded horse includes grooming and turn-out exercise. *Cf.* rough board.

full brothers/sisters
Horses having the same sire and dam. *See also* half brothers/sisters.

full cheek snaffle
See cheek.

full mouth
Having all the permanent teeth. A horse will grow from thirty-six to forty-four teeth: twenty-four molars, twelve incisors, and anywhere from none to four each of canine and wolf teeth.

full pass
A lateral movement in which the horse moves sideways with no forward motion. Also known as side pass. Used in dressage tests and as a general suppling exercise.

furlong
One-eighth of a mile or 220 yards, the standard unit of measurement for flat racing.

furosemide
A diuretic medication used to treat bleeding (which see) by shrinking the capillaries in the lungs, widely known under its trade name Lasix®.

futurity
(1) A stakes race for two year olds for which owners pay a nominating fee and then additional fees as the race approaches;
(2) Any of certain horse show competitions for three year olds.

gag snaffle
A snaffle bit attached to a cheekpiece that draws upward and pulls the bit's mouthpiece into the corners of the horse's mouth while simultaneously putting pressure on the poll. Widely used in polo and show jumping for its slowing and stopping power, it is considered a severe but by no means brutal piece of tack.

gait
One of the distinctive leg movements of a horse in motion. These include the walk, the jog or trot, the lope or canter, the gallop, and certain others such as the singlefoot, rack, pace, and fox trot.

gaited horses
The familiar collective term for American Saddlebreds and Tennessee Walking Horses, and sometimes including such other breeds as the Missouri Fox Trotter and Rocky Mountain Horse. The distinguishing feature is the horses' ability to move at other than the basic walk, trot, and canter.

Galiceño
The product of Spanish horses brought to North America by Cortez, the breed was used first in Mexico and then in the United States for ranch work and as pack horses. At under fourteen hands at maturity but nevertheless classified as a horse, the Galiceño is compact in build and possesses great stamina for an animal of its size.

gallop
(1) The horse's natural running gait;
(2) In racing, to exercise a horse, usually during the morning workout period.

Horses are born knowing how to gallop

(© CHERRY HILL)

galloping boot
In racing, a covering for the ankle, shin, and tendons that protects against abrasion caused by the racetrack surface.

Galwayne's (or Galvayne's) groove
The groove in the upper incisor teeth that grows longer as a horse ages. It appears when the horse is ten, reaches approximately

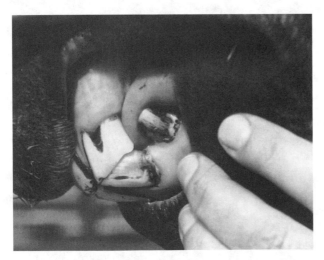

Galwayne's groove visible in the upper incisor of a twelve-year-old gelding

(© RICHARD KLIMESH)

halfway down the tooth by age fifteen, and reaches the bottom at age twenty. Named after the nineteenth-century British horseman Sydney Galwayne, the indentation is valuable in accurately estimating a horse's age.

gaskin
The part of the hind leg between the stifle and the hock.

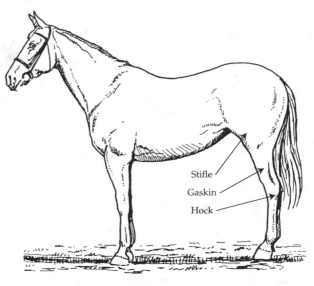

Stifle
Gaskin
Hock

Gaskin

gaucho
The "cowboy" horseman of Argentina and Brazil who work cattle on the vast *estancias*, or ranches.

geld
To castrate a male horse, which is then called a gelding. The procedure renders the animal easier to manage.

Gelderlander
A breed native to Gelder province of the Netherlands. Standing approximately sixteen

hands high and chestnut in color, the Gelderlander is used primarily for carriage driving.

gestation
The period between conception and birth, approximately eleven months for a horse.

get
The offspring of a stallion. The offspring of a mare is called produce.

gig
(1) A two-wheeled driving vehicle with a single seat;
(2) A Western term for spurring a horse.

girth
(1) The circumference of a horse's body behind its elbow;

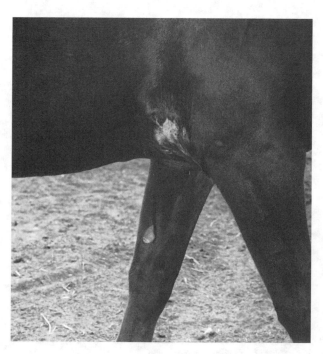

Girth gall

(© RICHARD KLIMESH)

(2) A strap that passes under a horse's belly to secure the saddle in place. The word usually describes the piece of English tack and the rear cinch on a Western saddle.

girth extender
A piece of tack that buckles onto the girth to increase its length.

girth gall or girth sore
A blister or raw sore caused by the continuous rubbing of an ill-fitting girth or cinch, treated by antiseptic and rest and preventable by tack that is correctly fitted and adjusted. Long-term aggravation may lead to a severe abscess. Treatment includes cleaning and dressing the wound (and draining any trapped pus or blood), followed by rest until the wound has healed. Properly fitting tack prevents the condition from occurring. Also known as cinch sore.

give tongue
Of a foxhound, to bark enthusiastically, especially when scenting a fox.

Godolphin Barb
Along with the Byerly Turk and Darley Arab, one of the three Thoroughbred foundation sires. The stallion was purchased in Paris by Edward Coke in 1729 (according to the story, the horse was discovered pulling a cart), who then took the horse to England. The horse was then acquired in 1733 by the Earl of Godolphin.

gogue (rhymes with *rogue*)
A type of martingale attachment that applies pressure to the horse's poll and bit. It is used to influence the animal's head and neck position.

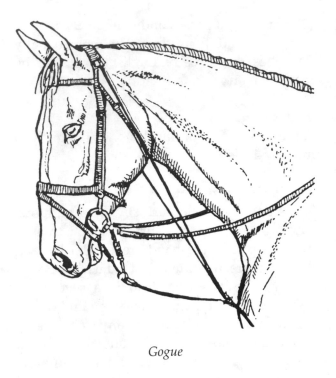
Gogue

going
See footing.

going away
In racing, winning by an ever-increasing margin as the horse approaches the finish line.

gone away
In foxhunting, when the fox leaves the covert.

good
In racing, a surface footing that is slightly damper and thus slightly slower-going than a fast track.

goose rump
A pronounced slope of the hindquarters from croup to dock. Many horsemen believe a goose rump indicates a horse with an aptitude for jumping.

go-round
In Western horse shows or rodeos, a sequence in which all or certain qualified entrants in the class or event compete.

go to ground
In foxhunting, a fox that disappears into a burrow or another hole is said to have gone to ground.

grab
A colloquial term for overreaching, as in "The horse grabbed himself in his near foreleg."

grade
A horse of no specific breed, the "mutt" of the horse world; also, a horse that will not be accepted for registration by a breed organization.

graded race
Races that have been categorized according to quality of horses and/or purse sizes. Grade I (abbreviated to GI) is the highest category, grade II (GII) the next, and so on to grade IV. Group races are the European equivalent and are indicated by Arabic, not Roman, numerals.

granddam
The mother of a horse's dam (also known as the "second dam").

Grand National
The well-known steeplechase race held each spring at the Aintree race course in Liverpool, England. The course is 4 miles 860 yards in length and includes thirty obstacles, including the formidable Beecher's Brook and The Chair, where many falls occur. Popularized by

the film *National Velvet,* the Grand National is widely considered the world's most difficult steeplechase.

grand prix
(1) A show jumping class involving the horse show's most demanding course and large amount of prize money;
(2) *Capitalized* an upper-level dressage test requiring such advanced movements as piaffe and passage. The phrase is French for "great [rich] prize."

Grand Prix Special
An upper-level dressage test involving more collected movements and more demanding sequences of movements than a Grand Prix (see above) does.

grandsire
The father of a horse's sire.

gray
A mixture of white hairs with any other colored hairs. Appearances to the contrary, there are no white horses (except for albinos, which are a genetic mutation); horses that seem to be white are in fact light gray.

grazing bit
A curb bit with rear-curving shanks, so-called because the shanks permit the horse to put its head closer to the ground than a curb bit with straight shanks would (some riders object to their horse's eating while working, while other riders do not).

green
(1) An untrained horse or one that is just beginning its training;

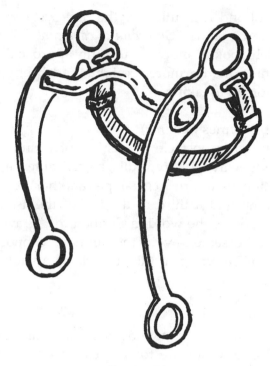

Grazing bit

(© CHERRY HILL 2000)

(2) The color of the prize ribbon awarded for sixth place.

green-broke
The minimum degree to which a horse has been trained to accept and respond to a rider.

green hunter
(1) A show hunter in its first or second year of showing, that is, First-Year Green or Second-Year Green;
(2) An American Quarter Horse that has not yet earned more than ten points in working hunter or jumping classes.

Grisone, Federico [precise dates unknown]
A sixteenth-century Italian horseman who, in Naples, established the first modern riding

school and the author of the first systematic training manual, *Gli ordini di cavalcare* (1550), which took a more systematic approach to training than armored knights had been accustomed to taking.

grob (rhymes with *rob*)
A jumping obstacle consisting of a sunken passageway with, typically, a vertical fence at the top of the descent slope, another at the bottom, and a third at the top of the ascent slope. Since the word is German for "grave," some horsemen avoid the ominous connotation by referring to the obstacle as a sunken road.

groom
As a noun, a person whose job is to clean, feed and otherwise care for horses; as a verb, to clean a horse.

ground hitched
Of a riderless horse, trained to stand with no more restraint than the ends of the reins touching the ground. The need for such discipline came from the lack of a fence, tree, or another object to which a cowboy could tie his horse when he needed to dismount, perhaps to examine a calf, out on the range.

ground line
In jumping, the actual or perceived base of a fence that a horse and rider will use to judge at which point to leave the ground.

ground rail
A pole of the size used to make jumping fences that is placed directly on the ground, to be walked, trotted, or cantered over. Ground

Walking over ground rails

rails are useful in helping a horse and rider learn to regulate the length of strides or how to see a distance.

groundwork
(1) The type of schooling when the trainer is standing on the ground, as distinguished from when the horse is being ridden;
(2) Training the horse "on the flat," as distinguished from being worked over fences.

grullo
A smoky or mouse-colored body color (not a mixture of black and white hairs, but each hair mouse-colored) with black mane and tail and usually a black dorsal stripe and black on lower legs.

gullet
On a Western saddle, the arched open part below the horn or pommel; on an English saddle, the center panel that runs the length of the saddle's underside.

gymkhana

A program of mounted games, such as pole bending and musical chairs. From a Hindu word for "ball-house," gymkhanas were a popular training exercise among British cavalrymen stationed in India and who then brought the idea back to Europe. The games are now a feature of Pony Club and other competitions in which youngsters take part.

gymnastic

In jumping, a series of low fences set at specific distances to encourage a horse to lengthen or shorten his stride. Gymnastic work also encourages a horse to use his back and hind legs and to jump in a balanced and athletic fashion.

habit

An outfit of clothes for riding, a term now used primarily to describe the coat and long skirt worn by sidesaddle riders.

hack

(1) A pleasure ride;
(2) The familiar term for an under-saddle hunter class.

hackamore

A bitless bridle that controls the horse by means of pressure from the bosal on the animal's nose. A mechanical hackamore has long metal shanks and a curb strap or chain that creates a curblike lever effect to tighten the bosal. Hackamores are most often seen on horses that have been schooled to neck-rein. *See* bosal, fiadore, and mecate.

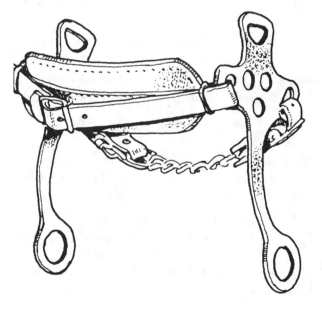

Mechanical hackamore

hack barn
A stable where horses are rented for pleasure rides.

Hackney
The name Hackney applies to a breed of horse and of pony. Both are noted for their high-stepping action at the walk and trot and, accordingly, are used for driving, especially in horse show classes. Both Hackney horses and ponies were developed in eighteenth-century England through the crossing of Thoroughbreds with trotting horses. The animals have relatively small heads, long and curved necks, and compact bodies of a solid color. In American horse shows, Hackney ponies are driven in four-wheeled roadster carts or in sulkies, and are judged primarily on their animated gaits at the walk and trot.

The word *Hackney* is thought to come from a French word for "nag." Hackney horses and the hired carriages they once pulled have lent their name to *hack* as a slang term for a taxicab.

Haflinger
The breed of pony originating in the Austrian Tyrol. Standing slightly under 14 hands and with a coat that ranges from chestnut to palomino, the sure-footed and hardy Haflinger is prized as a riding and driving animal. Members of this especially long-lived breed have had healthy and productive lives well into their forties.

half brothers/sisters
Horses having the same dam but different sires. *See also* full brothers/sisters.

half chaps
Leather chaps that extend from the rider's ankles to just below the knee. They are (literally) cooler to wear than full chaps.

half cheek snaffle
See cheek.

half halt
Application of the rider's hand and leg aids to get a momentary rebalancing from the horse or as a signal to the horse to prepare for a change of gait or pace. It is accomplished by a combination of the rider's applying hand and seat aids while maintaining impulsion with the legs, all done within a single stride.

half pass
A lateral movement in which the horse simultaneously moves sideways and forward.

Half pass in dressage

half school
The classical term for a change of direction while moving, made by reversing toward the center of the arena and thus making half of a figure-eight.

half seat
The hunter-seat equitation position where only the rider's lower legs are in contact with the horse; the rider's seat is up out of the saddle so that the horse's hind end will have less weight at the canter or gallop. Also known as two-point contact, the half seat is an excellent way for a rider to develop balance and leg strength.

halt
The term for asking a horse to stand still, or the position of a motionless horse.

halter
(1) The bridlelike apparatus used to lead or restrain a horse. Because hitching a horse by the reins can lead to a mouth injury if the horse rears back, using a halter is the customary way to secure a riderless horse;
(2) A term for a horse show conformation or breeding class.

Hambletonian.
See Standardbred.

hammerhead
An English spur with a blunt square neck.

hand
The unit by which horses are measured from their withers to the ground. One hand equals

Horse in halter

four inches, so a horse that stands fifteen hands high (abbreviated hh) measures sixty inches at the shoulder.

handicap
In racing (1) A race in which weights are assigned according to the horses' past performance and present form. The goal is to create a theoretical dead heat among all horses in the race;
(2) To determine the relative merits among the horses in a race by using such data as breeding, past performance, latest workouts, and record of recent successes of the horse's jockey and trainer;
(3) In polo, *see* rating.

handicapper
The racetrack official, usually the racing secretary, who assigns the weights that the horses will carry.

handily
In racing, winning easily, with little effort from the jockey.

handle
In racing, the total amount of money passing through the pari-mutuel machines for one race, the entire day's racing, or another period.

hand ride
In racing, urging the horse by the use of the jockey's hands and body weight without using the whip. A jockey will hand ride a horse that is winning so easily and eagerly that it needs no greater urging.

hands
The degree of skill and finesse with which a rider uses the reins. To have "good hands" is a high compliment.

hang a leg
Of a jumping horse, to let one foreleg dangle below the other over the top of the fence. Because it is an indication of an unsafe jumping style (the horse might hit that leg against the top of the obstacle), hunter class judges will penalize a horse that hangs a leg.

Hanoverian
A warmblood breed that originated in the eighteenth century in the German province of Hanover. The breed's solid body and powerful legs make Hanoverians excellent dressage and show jumping horses, their primary use today.

harness racing
Standardbred trotting and pacing racing, as distinguished from flat racing and steeplechasing.

haunches-in
A two-track movement in which the horse travels with his croup closer to the center of the ring than his shoulders are carried.

haute école
French for "high school."

hay
Dried grass fed primarily as a source of roughage. A horse at work requires approximately 1 percent of its body weight in fresh grass or hay, or a daily average of ten to fifteen pounds. Hay comes in two categories: legumes, which includes alfalfa and clover, produce nitrogen and are rich in protein and calcium; grasses, including timothy and red tip, are richer in carbohydrates. As a general rule, horses are fed a mixture of legume and grass hay to get the fullest benefit from this important dietary staple.

hay cubes
Hay that has been compressed into cube-shaped pellets. Packaged in easy-to-store bags, cubes lack the dust that regular hay can have, and so they are preferable for horses with heaves or other breathing or allergic conditions. However, cubes are more expensive than regular hay.

hay grass
Any of various species of grass rich in carbohydrates, as distinguished from protein-rich legumes.

hay net
A feeding container made of knotted string or light rope and suspended in a stall to hold a quantity of hay.

Hay net

hazard
In combined driving, a cross-country obstacle. Among the most popular with course designers are water hazards (ponds or streams through which the entries are driven) and mazes made of logs.

head
(1) To place a horse in front of a cow to stop or to force the cow to change directions;

(2) In racing, the margin between horses equal to the length of a head.

header
(1) In team roping, the contestant who ropes the steer's horns or head;
(2) In chariot racing, the assistant who makes sure the horses are facing straight ahead at the start of the race.

headstall
The Western bridle excluding the bit.

"heads up!"
The traditional warning to be aware of an approaching horse.

heat
(1) In racing, one of a series of qualifying races to determine eligibility in the finals of a race;
(2) Increased temperature in the leg that is capable of being felt as higher than normal. Detected by touch, heat is an indication of a possible injury or illness because of the increased blood flow that raises the temperature;
(3) The condition of a mare that is receptive for breeding: ovulating or in estrus; the mare is said to be "in heat".

heaves
A disease, similar to asthma in humans, marked by difficulty in breathing, coughing, and loss of energy. The cause is exposure to dust, molds, and other allergens. Changing the horse's environment and/or administering medication to help the animal breathe are the treatments. A horse that suffers from the condition is referred to as "heavy" (HEE-vy).

heavy
In racing, a track surface that is drying out, somewhere between muddy and good.

heavy on the forehand
Of a horse, unbalanced because it is carrying too much of its body's weight on its forequarters, which restricts the ability to move forward with optimum impulsion. The solution is a half halt or more prolonged combination of rein and driving aids.

heel
The rear portion of the foot.

heeler
In team roping, the contestant who ropes the steer's hind legs.

herring-gutted
A conformation fault marked by flat sides that extend sharply from girth to stifle.

high hooking (or high sticking)
In polo, a foul in which the player lifts the head of his mallet above his shoulder and then makes contact with an opponent.

high school
The translation of the French phrase *haute école*, referring to the most advanced dressage movements, such as passage, piaffe, and airs above the ground.

hind
Short for hind foot, hind leg, or hindquarters.

hindquarters
The portion of the horse behind the barrel.

hinney
The offspring of a horse and a female ass.

hippology
The study of horses, ponies, and other equines.

hitch
(1) The device on the back of a truck or another towing vehicle to which the trailer is attached;
(2) To fasten a horse to a driving vehicle;
(3) To tie a horse to a post, tree, or another stationary object to keep the horse from wandering off.

hobble
A restraining strap attached to a horse's legs to keep it from wandering off (not to be confused with hopple).

hock
The joint of the hind leg between the gaskin and the cannon bones. The equivalent of the

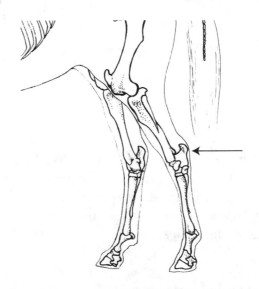

Hock

(© CHRISTINA BERUBE)

human knee, the hock is the source of a horse's "rear engine" impulsion.

hog
To cut a mane shorter than a roached mane.

hog-tie
To tie a calf or steer by three legs after the animal has been thrown down. Such a tie marks the end of a calf roping go-round.

"hold hard!"
In foxhunting and elsewhere in the horse world, the command to come to an immediate halt.

hold out
In jumping, to remain on the track (usually along the arena's rail) until the horse is lined up with a fence set inside the track. Lining up a jump permits the most direct straight route to the obstacle.

Holsteiner
A warmblood breed that originated in the seventeenth century in the German province of Holstein. Originally a coach horse, the Holsteiner benefited from subsequent infusions of Thoroughbred blood to become a valuable dressage and show jumping horse.

homebred
A horse bred by its owner or in the breeder's home state.

home stretch
See stretch.

Honorary Secretary
In foxhunting, the official who sends out fixture cards, collects capping fees, and performs other of the hunt's administrative duties.

hood
A covering worn over the horse's head and neck to protect the animal from dirt or from insects.

Hood

hoof
The hard outside part of the foot. Like the human fingernail, the horse's hoof must be trimmed when it grows too long, a chore that usually must be done every six to eight weeks. Horses wear metal shoes that protect their hooves from pavement, rocks, and other hard surfaces and objects. Hooves are made of keratin, a protein substance, which dogs find

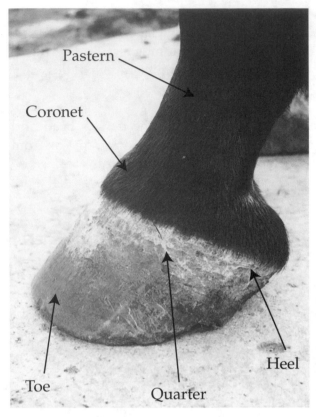

Hoof, side view

(© RICHARD KLIMESH)

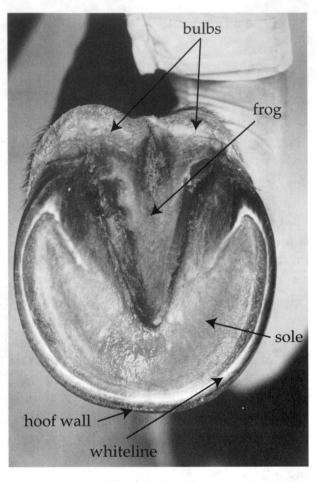

Hoof, bottom view

(© RICHARD KLIMESH)

tasty (which is why barn dogs gather around a blacksmith who is trimming hooves).

hoof dressing
A petroleum compound applied to moisturize dry hooves and to treat certain foot conditions. The substance also has cosmetic use; hooves of a show horse are painted with dressing right before entering the arena.

hoof pick
A hooked metal tool used for cleaning wadded hay, bedding, small stones, and so forth from the underside of the hoof.

hook
A sharp protrusion on a cheek tooth, routinely filed away by floating.

hooking
In polo, the legal tactic of reaching with the mallet head to catch the head of an opponent's mallet.

hoolihan
A toss of the lariat without any preliminary swings of the rope over the roper's head. (The

word is likely to be the name of a cowboy who had mastered the technique.).

hopples
In harness racing, leather straps worn on the legs of pacers to keep them from breaking into a trot or gallop.

horn
(1) The upright projection on the front of a Western saddle, especially designed to wrap a rope (*see* dally);
(2) The short instrument (the hunting horn) blown by the huntsman to signal hounds and the foxhunters, or the longer instrument (the coach horn) blown by some horse show ring-masters to signal the beginning of a class.

The horn of this saddle is wrapped with a band of rubber to prevent the rope from slipping

(© CHERRY HILL)

horse gentler
A term for a practitioner of resistence-free training. To gentle a horse is in contrast to the former practice of breaking a horse by harsher methods, such as outlasting the animal's bucking.

horseman
A person of either gender who has a thorough working knowledge of riding and horse care. Although the term *horsewoman* is widely used, few if any people object to the collective term *horsemen.*

horsemanship
Riding skill, especially with regard to form and control.

hot
Excitable.

hot blood
All or mostly Thoroughbred or Arabian. The phrase derives from the high-mettled ex-citable nature of such breeds and types. *Cf.* warmblood; cold blood.

hot shoeing
The method of making or fitting shoes by heating them in a forge. *Cf.* cold shoeing.

hot walker
A person or a machine that leads a sweating horse after exercise until the animal is cool. The hot-walker machine, to which one or more horse is attached to long vanes, is pow-ered by a small motor and leads the animal(s) around in a circle, thus freeing humans to do other duties.

hound
A canine used for foxhunting, the foxhound.

hunt cap
A sturdy velvet-covered headwear tradition-ally worn by the Master of Foxhounds and hunt staff and by competitors in hunter-seat

horse show classes and at lower levels of dressage and eventing. Like any other protective headgear, the cap should include a well-fitting chin harness.

Hunt cap

hunter

A horse show division in which horses are judged on their style of moving and jumping ability suitable for the foxhunting field: a ground-covering stride and an athletic and tidy form over fences. The term also applies to a horse or a person involved in the sport of foxhunting.

hunter clip

A pattern in which all the horse's body hair is trimmed except for a patch below the saddle (to absorb sweat) and the lower legs (to protect against thorns).

hunter hack

A horse show class in which horses are first judged over two low fences and then at the walk, trot, and canter.

hunter/jumper

English-style riding and showing that involves training and exhibiting hunters and jumpers, as distingished from saddle seat, combined training, dressage, and so forth.

hunter pace

A competition in which teams of two or three riders cover a cross-country course of several miles. The winner is the team that completes the course closest to the optimum time as established by the event's organizers.

hunter trial

A competition in which horses are judged over a cross-country course of fences on the athletic ability needed by foxhunting mounts.

hunter under saddle

A horse show class in which the horse is judged on its ability to move at the walk, trot,

Hunter under saddle class
(© AMERICAN QUARTER HORSE ASSOCIATION)

and canter as a hunter-type horse. Judges look for a ground-covering walk, a long, low daisy-cutter trot without breaking at the knee, and a smooth canter. Manners will also be taken into consideration.

hunt seat
The English-style riding position designed for jumping; also known as hunter seat.

hunt-seat equitation (also hunter-seat equitation)
A horse show class in which riders are judged on the form and control of their hunt-seat horsemanship.

huntsman
The member of a foxhunt's staff who is responsible for working the pack of hounds and supervising kennel activities. The Master of Foxhounds often acts in this capacity.

hunt staff
In foxhunting, the huntsman and whippers-in.

hurdle
A jumping race in which the obstacles are brush-topped bundles of sticks. The name comes from portable fencing once used to separate fields in which sheep were kept.

hybrid
The product of the mating of a horse and another equine species, such as an ass or zebra. Hybrids are almost always sterile.

Hyperkalemic Periodic Paralysis (HPP)
A muscular disorder that is an inherited affliction of certain American Quarter Horse bloodlines. Symptoms include twitching or tremors, sweating, and hind-end weakness or collapse. Because there is no known cure, efforts have been made to eliminate the bloodlines through selective breeding.

Icelandic horse
The breed of pony native to Iceland. (Although standing thirteen hands high or less, the breed is referred to as horse in Iceland.) It may well be the world's purest breed because no outside blood has been added since around the year 1200. It moves at five gaits: the walk, trot, gallop, pace, and the *tolt*, the comfortable running walk for which the breed is famous. Icelandic horses are among the world's most rugged, able to thrive on the island's sparse vegetation and able to cover great distances over the most demanding terrain with no discernable effort.

identification
A system of recognizing and verifying horses by means of several items that are noted on registration certificates, such as the animals' coat color, markings, lip markings, pattern of the chestnuts, scars, and brands.

impulsion
Energy generated by the horse's hindquarters to produce a forward thrust.

in-and-out
In jumping, a combination of two fences set one cantering stride, or approximately twenty-four feet, apart. The combination comes from foxhunting, where horses might be asked to jump over a fence out of a field, across a country lane, and over a second fence into the next field.

independent seat
A rider's ability to hold a proper body position without relying on the reins for support.

indirect rein
Rein pressure created by the rider drawing his hand back toward his opposite hip, used to

straighten or turn the horse by displacing the animal's weight. An example would be the rider's drawing the right rein toward his left hip, thus causing the horse to shift its hind-end to the left.

influenza
A highly contagious viral disease. As with humans, symptoms include coughing, muscle soreness, loss of appetite, and a decreased resistance to secondary infections. Vaccination reduces the chance of contracting the disease, for which rest is the primary treatment.

in front of the rider's leg
Of a horse, moving with enough impulsion to give the rider the feeling that the animal is ahead of and carrying the rider, as opposed to the feeling that the source of energy is lagging behind.

In gate
The entrance to an arena. Large arenas have both In and Out gates to avoid traffic congestion, while smaller rings use a single gate for both entrances and exits. In gates are traditionally where horse-show participants gather to watch the action in the company of other like-minded people.

in hand
Held or worked by someone who is standing on the ground. *In hand* is also another term for a halter class.

inquiry
In racing, an investigation instituted by the stewards to see whether a foul was committed. *See also* objection.

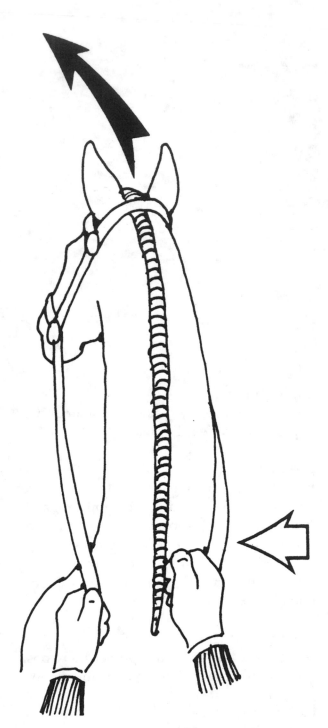

Indirect rein

(© CHERRY HILL 2000)

inside
(1) The side of the horse or rider that is closer to the center of a riding ring or arena. The left side would be the inside when a horse is traveling counterclockwise;
(2) In racing, a position closer or closest to the track rail.

interval training
A system of conditioning in which the horse is given increasingly more rigorous exercise immediately followed by rest periods to allow the animal's heart rate and lungs to recover, as a way to increase stamina.

invitational
A race or horse show class open only to those horses that have been asked to take part.

Irish Draft Horse
A native breed of Irish heavy horse. Although called a draft horse, the breed is far smaller and lighter than the Clydesdale, Percheron, or other draft breeds that are larger due to the infusion of Arab and Thoroughbred blood. Standing between sixteen and seventeen hands and with bone and substance, the Irish draft horse is a steady and agile jumper, which makes it suitable for breeding to Thoroughbreds to produce the Irish hunter, a crossbred used primarily as a foxhunting mount.

irons
The colloquial word for stirrups on an English or racing saddle.

jack spavin
A visible bone spavin.

jail
In racing, the thirty-day period after a horse has been claimed during which time it must run for a claiming price 25 percent higher than the price for which it was claimed.

jibbah
The characteristic bulge on an Arabian horse's forehead.

jig
An uncomfortable jerky and bobbing part-walk/part-jog trot. Horses often jig when excited or just feeling good.

jockey
(1) A rider in a horse race;
(2) To maneuver a horse during a race.

Jockey Club
The regulatory body of Thoroughbred racing. There are Jockey Clubs in every country that has such racing, with functions that include maintaining the stud book, accepting and approving registration and names of foals, and providing officials as stewards or judges.

jockey's agent
A representative of a jockey hired to arrange mounts for the rider. An agent is said to hold the jockey's book.

jodhpur boots
Low footwear secured with an ankle strap and traditionally worn with jodhpurs.

jodhpurs
English riding pants that extend to the ankle, worn by riders of gaited horses and by young children. The name comes from the Indian

province (now state) of Jodphur, where the native dress included similar leggings.

jog

The Western term for *trot*, especially a slow collected trot. Riders sit to the jog, but they post to what Westerners call the long trot.

Jumper class
(© WYATT MCSPADDEN/AMERICAN
QUARTER HORSE ASSOCIATION)

Jog
(© CHERRY HILL)

jousting

Today, a sport in which galloping riders try to spear a small ring suspended six to eight feet above the ground. Inspired by the activity of medieval knights in armor, jousting is the state sport of Maryland.

jumper

A horse show division in which horses are scored on their ability to clear fences and other obstacles without regard to the form or style of horse or rider. Also known as show jumping.

jumping derby

A demanding show jumping competition where the permanent course includes banks, sunken roads, and other natural obstacles.

jump-off

In show jumping, an additional tie-breaking round.

junior

A rider below the age of eighteen.

juvenile

In racing, a two year old. Races for juveniles are usually sprints so the young animals are not overtaxed

keeper
A leather loop on bridles and saddles in which the end of a strap is inserted to keep the end from flapping.

Kentucky Derby
The first of the Triple Crown races, held on the first Saturday in May at Churchill Downs, Louisville, Kentucky. First held in 1875 and run at a distance of a mile and a quarter, the Derby is arguably the most famous horse race in the United States.

Kimberwicke
A snaffle bit with a mouthpiece shaped into a low port. The Kimberwicke combines the actions of the snaffle and curb by means of a single set of reins.

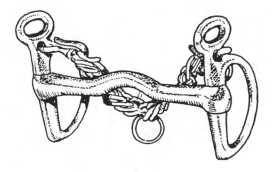

Kimberwicke bit

knee
The joint in the foreleg between the forearm and cannon bone.

knee roll
The padding on some English saddles against which the rider's knee is braced for support.

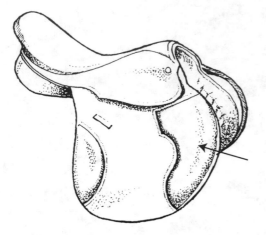

Knee roll

kur (KUHR)
A freestyle dressage competition performed to music that has been selected by the rider. The word is German for *choice*.

La Guérinière, François Robichon de (La GAIR-in-ee-yair) [1688–1751]
French horseman and author, an influential contributor to classical horsemanship. An adherant of the idea of school riding for its own sake (not just as training for the cavalry), he is credited with the invention of the shoulder-in, flying change or lead, and counter-canter.

laminitis
An inflammation and separation of the laminae, the parts of the foot that attach the wall of the hoof to the coffin bone, due to faulty blood circulation. In some cases the coffin bone begins to rotate. A major cause is overeating, especially rich food, or drinking cold water immediately after exercise. Other causes include stress, other ailments, and obesity. Treatments include long-term and total rest, anti-inflammatory medication,

Hooves of a horse with chronic laminitis
(© RICHARD KLIMESH)

and corrective shoeing. Chronic laminitis is known as founder.

landau
In driving, a four-wheeled two-seat vehicle with a folding top; named after a town in Germany.

Lasix®
See furosemide.

lateral movement
Any movement, such as the half-pass or the two-track, in which the horse moves simultaneously forward and to the side (the exception is the full or side pass, with no forward movement).

latigo (LAT-ig-oh)
The strap that fastens the cinch on a Western saddle.

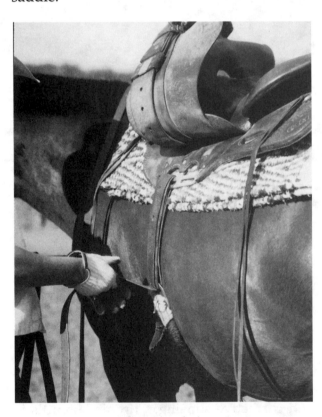

Adjusting a latigo

(© RICHARD KLIMESH)

lay up
To send a horse for rest or recuperation, or the period of such recovery.

lead (LEED)
The foreleg that consistently and most visibly precedes the other foreleg in striking the ground at the canter/lope and the gallop. When traveling counterclockwise, the horse should be on its left lead, and on the right lead in the other direction for optimal support and balance.

Determining which lead the horse takes is the responsibility of the rider, who applies the appropriate aids (or cues) to ask for that gait. *See* counter-canter; cross-canter; flying change of lead; simple change of lead; and wrong lead.

leader(s)
In driving, the horse(s) hitched in front of the others. *See* wheeler(s).

leading rein
See opening rein.

lead pony
In racing, a ridden horse (not a pony) that escorts race horses to the post. Being led in this fashion tends to reassure and relax the runners.

leak
Of a cutting horse, to lose the advantage over a cow by moving toward the animal instead of staying back and waiting for the cow to move forward.

leaning into a distance
Of a jumping rider, inclining one's upper body too far forward during the approach to a fence. Leaning increases the likelihood of being out of balance when the horse leaves the ground. *See* distance.

leaning on the bit
The effort by a horse to have its forequarters supported by the rider's hands, as opposed to carrying itself without such help.

leaping horn
The hooklike projection on a sidesaddle over which the rider rests her forward leg.

leathers
See stirrup leathers.

leave off a leg
Of a jumping horse, to leave the ground with one foreleg noticeably trailing the other. This unbalanced position, which can lead to the horse's hitting the fence or falling on landing, can be caused by the rider's restraining the animal's head at the take-off point.

leave out a stride
In jumping, to decrease by one the number of strides between two fences, accomplished by increasing the horse's length of stride. Its purpose is typically to save time in a jumper class. *See* add a stride.

left behind
In jumping, the rider's being thrown backward and thus out of position by the horse's jump; also called getting left.

legume
Any of the nitrogen-rich grasses used for hay, such as alfalfa.

leg up
(1) A boost into the saddle by someone standing on the ground, as jockeys are hoisted onto their horses;

(2) To exercise a horse in order to bring him back to peak condition, usually done after a horse has been laid up. *See* lay up.

leg wraps
Protective cloth material that snuggly encircles a horse's legs for support or to prevent injuries.

leg yield
Any lateral movement in which the inside fore- and hind legs cross in front of the outside legs. An example would be the two-track or the full pass.

leopard Appaloosa
An Appaloosa (which see) with dark spotted markings all over its body.

lespedeza
A legume grass used for hay.

levade
The air above the ground in which the horse bends its haunches and raises its forehand

Levade

until its body reaches and maintains a forty-five degree angle.

liberty horse
A riderless circus horse that performs in a group, doing such movements as circling around the ring or rearing on a command from the trainer who stands in front of them.

ligament
Fibrous tissue that connects bones as well as supporting and strengthening joints.

light horse
An obsolete British expression for a saddle horse that was not a pony or a draft or draft-cross horse. Light horses were used by the cavalry where speed was essential.

limit
A class for riders or horses that have not won more than three classes in that division at recognized horse shows.

line
In jumping, a series of two or more fences set apart at related distances.

linseed meal
A meal made from flax seeds, used as a laxative or a source of protein.

Lipizzaner (LIPPIT-zahner)
The Austrian breed most widely known for its association with the Spanish Riding School. The breed was created from Spanish horses imported to Austria in the sixteenth century. Between fifteen and sixteen hands high, stocky in build, and usually light gray in

Lipizzaners performing a quadrille
(© TEMPEL FARMS)

color, Lipizzaners are used for classical dressage and to a lesser extent for driving.

Little Brown Jug
See Standardbred.

live foal (or live foal guaranteed)
A provision in a breeding contract whereby the stud fee is due only if and when the mare delivers a live foal.

liver chestnut
A dark chestnut coat, the color of fresh raw liver.

Liverpool
A jumping obstacle composed of one or more rails over a shallow tray of water, named for such a fence at Aintree, Liverpool, the site of the Grand National steeplechase.

Llanero (YAH-nairo)
A native breed of Venezuela descended from Spanish stock. Slightly smaller than other Central and South American breeds, with an arched neck and small feet, the Llanero is widely used for ranch work.

local hunter
A horse show class open only to hunters that live within (usually) fifty miles of the show. The underlying reason is to exclude better horses from farther away from competing against and defeating animals from the show's vicinity.

lockjaw
See tetanus.

loin
The part of the back between the saddle and the croup. *See* coupling.

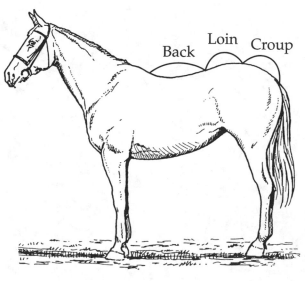

Loin

long
In jumping, a take-off spot that is uncomfortably far away from the obstacle, the opposite of tight or deep.

longe; lunge (LUNGE)
To exercise a horse by making it circle around its handler at the end of a rope that is fifteen feet or longer. Encouragement may come from a longe whip, five feet long and with a five-foot lash. Being longed is often done as a warm-up exercise for a horse or for a rider to develop a deep secure seat with or without stirrups and without the use of reins.

Longe

long reining
The procedure in which the trainer walks behind the horse and guides the animal with driving reins. Although used to teach a horse to be driven in harness, long reining is also used to school young horses before they are ridden. Also known as ground driving.

long trot
A Western term for an extended or rapid trot, as distinguished from the slower and more

comfortable jog. Western riders usually post the long trot and sit to the jog.

lope
A slow or collected three-beat gait, the Western term for the gait called the canter by English riders.

lop eared
Having ears that naturally flop downward and to the side.

lose
Of a cutting horse, to allow the selected cow to escape and return to the herd. Losing a cow will be heavily penalized in cutting horse competitions.

loss of use
An equine insurance contract provision providing for compensation in the event the horse cannot take part in its intended activity.

lower leg
The rider's leg from calf to anklebone.

Lusitano
The native breed of Portugal, virtually identical in comformation to the Andalusian and, like that breed, used as a riding and a carriage horse.

Lusitano performing the Spanish walk

m

maiden
(1) A horse of either sex than has never won a race;
(2) A horse show division for horses or riders that have not won a class in that division at a recognized show.

mane comb
A small metal comb with relatively wide spaces between the tines, used to clean a mane without breaking off the hairs.

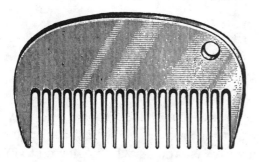
Mane comb

manège (MA-negzh)
An enclosure, usually covered, for training horses and riders. By extension, the word can apply to formal school dressage in general. The word comes from the French for "enclosure," from the same root as the word *menagerie*.

manège movements
See school movements.

marathon
The cross-country phrase of combined driving. Distances can range up to seventeen miles and include such hazards as ponds and maze-line gates.

mare
A female horse four years or older, or a female horse of any age that has given birth.

Marengo
The gray Arabian stallion ridden by Napoleon Bonaparte at the Battle of Waterloo. The horse was named for the town in Italy where in 1800 Napoleon defeated the Austrian army.

markings
The pattern of (usually) white hair on a horse's head and legs that help in identification. Common patterns include blaze, snip, star, socks and stockings.

martingale
A strap attached from the girth and running between the horse's forelegs to either the cavesson (standing martingale) or the reins (running martingale). A martingale is used to restrict a horse's head movement and thus increase the rider's control. *Cf.* tie-down.

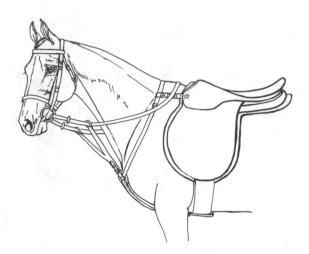

Running martingale

(© CHERRY HILL 2000)

mask
In foxhunting, the fox's head, awarded to a member of the field who is close to the hounds at the kill.

Master of Fox Hounds (MFH)
The presiding official of a foxhunt, who often assumes financial responsibility for the upkeep of the hounds and other expenses.

match race
A challenge race between two horses, most often between two celebrated horses to determine which is the better of the two.

maternal grandsire
The sire of a horse's dam.

Standing martingale (Western type)

(© CHERRY HILL)

mash
Crushed bran mixed with hot water and served warm to aid bowel regulation or post-exercise digestion. Mash is also given to horses with poor teeth.

maverick
An unbranded and unclaimed calf. The word comes from Samuel Maverick, a nineteenth-century Texas rancher who neglected to brand his cattle.

McClellen saddle

A saddle with a flexible tree, designed by Civil War General George McClellen to fit a wide range of horses. The saddle was and is used primarily by the cavalry and mounted police.

mecate (meh-KAT-ay)

The portion of some hackamores that ties to the back of the bosal and acts as reins.

medication list

In racing, a list kept by the track veterinarian and made available to identify horses that have been treated with permissible medication.

military

A European term for three-day eventing. The name comes from eventing's cavalry origins.

Miniature Horse

Reputed to be the world's smallest equine, the breed was created by the Falabella family of Argentina by inbreeding Shetland ponies for size. Standing only thirty inches at the shoulder when full grown, Miniature Horses are kept as pets or as harness ponies.

minus pool

In racing, a pari-mutuel betting pool that happens when a horse is so heavily bet on that, after state and track deductions, there is not enough money in the pool to pay the legally prescribed minimum amount on each winning bet. In such case, money from the track or the state racing association pays the difference.

Missouri Fox Trotter

An American breed noted for its fox trot, a comfortable sliding gait in which the horse walks in front and trots with its hind legs coming well underneath its body. Similar to other gaited horses, the purpose was to be able easily to carry a rider over rough terrain. The breed, which was developed in the nineteenth century, is also noted for its flat topline, powerful hindquarters, and amiable disposition.

mixed sale

A sale consisting of more than one type of horses, such as yearlings, broodmares, and horses in training.

mobile starting gate

In harness racing, a car or another vehicle with a long barrier mounted across its rear end. The horses trot or pace up to the barrier as the vehicle moves so that the horses get an even start on gait as they and the vehicle cross the starting line. The vehicle then accelerates away.

model

A horse-show term for a conformation or halter class.

modern pentathlon

See pentathlon.

Monday morning disease

See azorturia.

monkey mouth

The conformation fault of an undershot upper jaw. *Cf.* parrot mouth.

moon blindness

An inflammation of the iris in the eyeball. The severe pain causes the horse to blink, tear, and rub the eye. If untreated, blindness is likely.

Treatment includes antibiotic or cortisone oint- ment and confinement in subdued lighting. Known more formally as periodic opthalmia or recurrent uveitis, the term *moon blindness* refers to the old belief that the disease's recurrence was somehow related to phases of the moon.

Morab

A Morgan/Arab crossbred. Morabs make es- pecially good mounts for endurance riding and other long-distance activities.

Morgan

A breed of horse that originated in New Eng- land in the late eighteenth century. The foun- dation sire, thought to be a Thoroughbred, was named Figure and owned by a Vermont schoolteacher named Justin Morgan (the horse was often referred to as Justin Morgan, too). Figure matured into a stallion that was a compact but powerful saddle and driving horse that also hauled timber and pulled a plow. In addition, he became a remarkably

Morgan

(© JAN SYNICK/AMERICAN MORGAN HORSE ASSOCIATION)

prepotent sire, endowing his get with his conformation and his speed and stamina.

The Morgan has retained the crested neck and compact and well-rounded body, as well as great versatility as a riding and driving horse. In fact, the Justin Morgan class at horse shows requires the same horse to perform under saddle, in harness, and pulling weight.

morning glory
In racing, the sarcastic expression for a horse whose performances during races never equal its morning workout times.

morning line
In racing, the odds on a horse as determined by the track handicapper based on his or her estimation of odds likely to be determined by the bettors.

morning workout
In racing, the exercise period that lasts from dawn until mid- or late morning. Then the track is closed to prepare for the day's racing.

motion
The rider's upper body position in relation to the horse's center of gravity. A rider who is in balance with the horse is said to be riding "with the motion." Riding "behind the motion" is appropriate when using the driving aids to encourage the horse forward. Riding "ahead of the motion" disturbs the horse's balance by placing too much of the rider's weight on the animal's forehand.

mount fee
In racing, the flat fee earned by a jockey who has not ridden any of the top three finishers in a race (when he would have earned a percentage of the purse).

mounting block
A cement or wooden elevation used to facilitate getting on a horse.

move up
In jumping, to ask the horse to extend its stride and cover more ground with each stride, done when the distance to the take-off spot appears too far away from the fence.

muck out
To clean a stall of manure and soiled bedding.

mudder
In racing, a horse that performs well on a wet track.

muddy
In racing, a track surface that is soft and wet but without pools of water, as distinguished from sloppy.

mud knot
A loose knot tied in a horse's tail. The shorter length keeps as much mud as possible out of the tail hair. Mud knots are most often seen on horses that race on rainy days.

mule
The offspring of a jackass and a mare (cf. hinney, which is the offspring of a horse and a female ass). Standing approximately 15 hands tall, mules are used primarily as pack animals, although they can be used for riding and occasionally appear in horse shows and dressage competitions. Like hinnies (and most

other inter-species crosses), mules are almost always sterile.

mullen mouth

A snaffle bit having a mouthpiece with ridge-like indentations that act against the horse's tongue with more effect than a straight mouthpiece would.

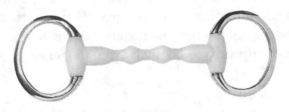

Mullen mouth bit
(© MILLER HARNESS COMPANY L. L. C.)

mustang

The wild horse native to the Western United States. Descended from escaped or stolen Spanish horses brought to North America during the colonial era, the present-day mustang is a small (approximately fifteen hands) and rugged animal that continues to roam the West's remaining rangeland in herds.

mutton-withered

The conformation defect of poorly defined, flat withers.

muzzle

The part of the face between the nostrils and the upper lip.

narky
Of a horse, behaving in an erratically uncooperative manner, as if under the influence of narcotics or other mood-altering drugs. A slang and perjorative term.

Narragansett Pacer
A now-extinct breed developed in colonial New England. Its influence can be still found in such breeds as the Standardbred, Morgan, and Saddlebred. According to legend, Paul Revere rode a Narragansett Pacer on his famous midnight ride.

National Show Horse
A breed composed of Arabian/Saddlebred crossbreds. Standing approximately sixteen hands high, the horses have gracefully arched necks, fine features, and elevated and elegant gaits.

Nations Cup
An international team show-jumping competition involving two rounds of jumping. The three best scores of each team's round (four horses customarily compete) count toward the overall scores.

natural aids
The rider's legs, hands (via the reins), seat, and voice. *See* aid; artificial aids.

navicular disease
A degenerative condition of the front feet caused by faulty blood flow to, or pressure on, the navicular bone and the surrounding area. This common cause of lameness appears as a choppy movement of one or both front feet. Treatment involves corrected shoeing to take the pressure off the front of the foot, anti-inflammatory medication, and reduced work.

near side

The left side of a horse. Because such activities as leading, mounting, and dismounting are done on or next to the horse's left side, that side is nearer the person doing the activity. (The tradition of mounting and dismounting on the near side arose in the days when men carried swords; most people were right-handed and carried their swords on their left hips, which made mounting and dismounting from the left side less cumbersome). *Cf.* off side.

neck

(1) the part of the body that connects the head to the shoulders;
(2) in racing, the margin between two horses equal to the length of a neck.

neck rein

Rein pressure created by one rein's pressing against the horse's neck, used as a cue to turn to the other side. For example, neck reining against the left side of the neck asks for a right turn. Western horses have been traditionally and routinely taught to neck rein so cowboys can ride one-handed, using their free hand to rope. Also known as bearing rein.

neck rope

In calf roping, a loop around a horse's neck through which one end of the rider's lasso passes from the saddle horn to the rider's hands. This arrangement acts as something of an anchor to keep the horse from running off after the roper dismounts.

neck shot

In polo, a stroke in which the player's mallet makes contact with the ball under the pony's neck. It is used primarily to send the ball at a

A neck shot

right angle to the direction in which the horse is traveling.

nerving

The largely obsolete procedure in which a nerve in the horse's leg is cut or removed; done to animals with lower leg or foot problems to eliminate pain. However, nerved horses would then work beyond the capacity of the affected limbs to do so safely, and the animals would break down.

Newcastle, William Cavendish, duke of
[1592–1676]
English military leader, riding master, and author. His book *Methode et Invention Nouvelle de dresser les Chevaux* advocated abandoning the

harsh training methods of the Renaissance in favor of a more gentle and understanding approach.

New Forest

A pony breed native to the New Forest area of Hampshire in England. The largest of the British native ponies, the New Forest stands up to 14.2 hands high, making it suitable to carry children and most adults.

Newmarket boots

Tall canvas and rubber boots designed to be worn in wet weather. The name comes from the English racing center of Newmarket.

Nez Percé horse

A crossbred of Appaloosa and Akhal-Teke, established as a breed in 1995 in an effort to restore the Appaloosa as originally created by the Nez Percé tribe. *See* Appaloosa.

nick

A merger of bloodlines that is likely to produce a desirable offspring, especially for racing.

night blindness

An inherited vision problem from which horses are virtually or actually blind in low light. Symptoms include a reluctance to move in the dark and cross-eyes when viewed from the front. There is no known cure.

night eye

Another name for chestnut (definition 2).

nod

In racing, a lowered head at the finish line that crosses the wire just ahead of another horse.

The expression "gets the nod" refers to a horse that wins in such a fashion. Also called bob.

nonpro

In Western horse showing, an amateur.

nose

(1) the front part of the head below the nostrils;
(2) in racing, the distance between race horses equal to the length of a nose, the shortest distance by which one horse can beat another.

novice

(1) the division for riders or horses that have not won more than three classes in that division at recognized horse shows;
(2) the introductory level of competition in recognized combined training and dressage events.

Number 1

In polo, the player whose primary function is to spearhead the drive on the opposing team's goal.

Number 2

In polo, the player whose primary function is to back up the Number 1 player.

Number 3

In polo, the player whose primary function is to direct the team's scoring attacks. Normally the team's best player plays the Number 3 position. *See also* back (definition 3).

numnah (NUM-na)

A British term for a saddlepad.

oats
A cereal grain widely used as feed.

objection
In racing, an inquiry made by a jockey, trainer, or owner before the race has been declared official that a horse had been interfered with during the running of the race. If the stewards sustain the objection, the order of finish will be altered accordingly. *See* inquiry.

obstacles
The final phase of a combined driving competition, in which vehicles negotiate a course of cone obstacles. Pairs of traffic cones set slightly wider than the vehicles' axles line the course. Tennis balls are balanced on the tops of the cones, and any ball that a vehicle dislodges results in penalty points. Also known as cones.

Obstacles phase of a combined driving competition

odds
In racing, an indication of how much money bettors will collect on a particular horse based on either handicappers' estimation of the horse's chance of winning (the morning line)

or the actual amounts of money bet on all the horses in that race. *See* pari-mutuel.

odds-on
Odds of less than even money, expressed as "one-to-ten," "three-to-five," and so on.

offset oxer
In jumping, a spread fence of which the rear element is lower than the front element. Offsets are illegal in schooling and competition on the grounds of a horse show because the optical illusion traps horses into hitting the back rail, although that is in fact the purpose of such fences in schooling. *See* bump.

offset stirrup
English stirrups with longer inside arms that cause the treads to slope inward. The purpose is to help riders keep the weight of their feet on the inside of the stirrup (although many trainers decry this "short cut" to proper position).

off side
The right side of a horse. *See* near side.

off stride
In harness racing, galloping instead of trotting or pacing. A horse that goes off stride must be pulled down to the trot or pace within several strides or else be disqualified.

off the pace
In racing, to run behind the leaders at the early stages of the race.

off-track betting
Wagering in legal outlets other than at the racetrack.

Oldenburg
A German Warmblood breed. Originally based on the Friesian horse, the Oldenburg was modified with infusions of Cleveland Bay, Hanoverian, and Thoroughbred blood until the horse became the largest in size of all the German Warmbloods. Standing between sixteen and seventeen hands high with a deep body, strong shoulders, and good bone, it is widely used as a show jumper.

Olympic Games
Equestrian events in this quadrennial international competition are show jumping, dressage, three-day eventing, and the riding phase of the modern pentathlon.

Olympic martingale
A training device composed of leather straps, one end of which is snapped onto the rings of a running martingale and passed through the bit rings; the other end is attached to the rein some twelve inches from the bit. The horse's raising his head higher than it should be causes the straps to pull downward on the bit and thus exert pressure on the animal's mouth.

one-sided
Of a horse, working more comfortably and effectively in one direction than the other. Because a one-sided horse is limited in athletic ability, such suppling exercises as the shoulder-in and leg yields are solutions to this problem.

on the bit
A description of a horse that is flexed, accepting the bit, responsive to the rider's aids, and moving with impulsion. Although the term comes from dressage, the concept is found in all equestrian disciplines.

on the muscle
Strong, or frisky.

open
(1) a class or division at the highest level of difficulty in that category, such as open equitation, in which riders who have won more than three classes in that division are eligible; (2) a class, division, or competition in which both professional and amateur or nonpro riders are eligible.

opening circle
In jumping, a wide circle made between entering the arena and approaching the first fence. Its purpose is to establish pace and impulsion. Also known as a courtesy circle.

opening rein
Pressure on the bit created by the rider's moving the rein hand out to the side away from

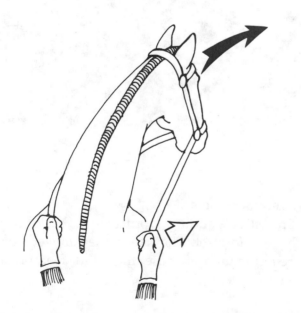

Opening rein used to turn the horse to the right

(© CHERRY HILL 2000)

the horse's shoulder, used to turn the horse in that direction without slowing his forward progress. Also known as leading rein.

orchard grass
A type of hay grass.

osslet
A bony growth on the outside of the ankle joint caused by a wound, bruise, or strain. Symptoms are puffiness of the fetlock joint, soft tissue, and/or lameness. If lameness persists, the osslet may need to be surgically removed.

out of
A horse's maternal relationship. "Secretariat was out of Somethingroyal" indicates that Somethingroyal was Secretariat's mother.

out-of-hand release
In jumping, a release in which the rider's hands follow the horse's head from takeoff to landing. The reins remain in a direct line from the rider's elbows to the horse's mouth. *Cf.* crest release.

out of the money
In racing, finishing worse than third. So-called because bettors do not win money on a horse that finishes worse than third.

outrider
In racing, the mounted escort that leads the field to the starting gate and, in flat or steeple-chase racing, catches the loose horse of a jockey who is thrown before or during a race.

outside
(1) the side closer to the rail of a riding ring or arena; the right leg of a rider who is moving

counterclockwise around a ring is the outside leg;

(2) in racing, a position away from the track's inner rail.

over at the knee
A conformation defect in which the upper leg arches forward from the knee when viewed from the side.

overbent
Of a horse, being asked to turn or being bent as a suppling exercise, moving forward with too much sideways bend from poll to tail. The rider's coordinating rein and leg aids will correct this position.

overface
In jumping, to present a horse at a fence or another obstacle that is too high or otherwise too difficult for that particular animal to attempt successfully. Overfacing a horse is a quick way to create long-term problems with regard to refusals and other disobediences.

overflexed
Too much bend at the poll, as indicated by the horse's face carried behind the vertical. The correction is to relax rein pressure while applying or maintaining the driving aids.

overgirth
See surcingle (definition 2).

overlay
In racing, higher odds than, in the handicapper's opinion, the horse's past performance would suggest. An overlay is considered a good bet.

overmounted
Riding a horse that is too difficult for that rider's ability.

overnight
In racing, a race for which entries close seventy-two hours or less before the first race on the day that particular race is to be run. Such a time frame allows trainers to make last-minute decisions about whether to enter their horses.

overo (OH-vairo)
A Paint or pinto coat of a dark color with white patches. The opposite is tobiano, which is a white coat with dark patches.

Overo

(© RICHARD KLIMESH)

overreach boots
Protective padding worn on the backs of a horse's forefeet. They keep the forefeet from being injured in case the hind feet brush against them.

overreaching
See forging.

oxbow

A relatively narrow Western stirrup with a rounded bottom.

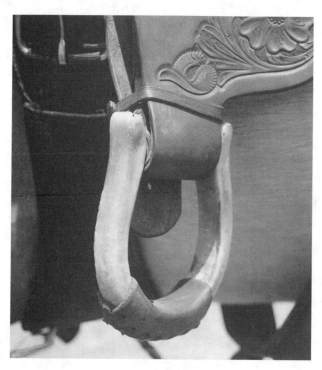

Oxbow stirrup

(© RICHARD KLIMESH)

oxer

In jumping, an obstacle made of two or more sets of standards to create width. *See* step oxer; offset oxer. Although a Liverpool and water jump test the ability to jump width, they are not considered oxers. The word comes from the reluctance of oxen and other bovines to jump width, the reason why double fences were used to separate fields.

Oxer

pace

A two-beat lateral gait natural to some Standardbreds (pacers) and, with some variations, to the Paso Fino and certain other breeds. The right foreleg and hind leg move simultaneously, as do the left foreleg and hind leg. The tendency to pace is largely inherited, although training can develop and enhance the ability. *See* amble.

packer

A horse with a kind temperament, one that will carry an inexperienced or inept rider safely and without objection.

pad

(1) a fabric blanket worn between the saddle and the horse's back to cushion the back against the weight of the saddle and rider and also to absorb sweat;

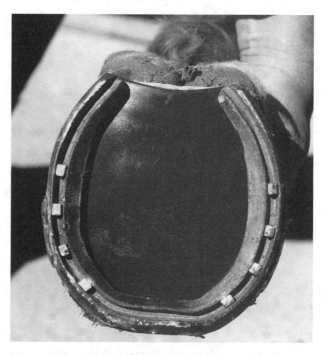

Pad for hoof

(© RICHARD KLIMESH)

121

(2) a hard plastic or rubber sheet that covers and protects the sole of the foot against rocks and other hard objects.

paddling
An undesirable movement in which one or more feet swing to the outside similar to the motion of a canoe paddle. Also known as paddling out.

paddock
(1) in racing, the enclosure where horses are saddled before a race;
(2) a fenced area in which horses are turned out for free exercise or rest.

paddock boots
Low laced or zipped riding footwear. *Cf.* jodhpur boots, which are secured by straps.

Paddock boots
(© MILLER HARNESS COMPANY L. L. C.)

Paint
The American breed having patches of white and another color above its knee and also having at least one parent registered with the American Paint Horse Association, the Jockey Club (Thoroughbreds) or the American Quarter Horse Association. Although Paints and pintos resemble each other in coloration, the distinction is in their ancestry.

pair
In driving, two horses hitched side by side.

palfrey
A light riding horse of the Middle Ages and Renaissance that paced or ambled.

palomino
Any horse having a golden yellow coat with white mane and tail; *capitalized* a member of that registered breed. As a color type (as distinguished from a breed), palomino individuals appear in many breeds, such as the American Quarter Horse and Paso Fino. The most prized hue is the color of a newly minted gold coin.

Pan American Games
The equestrian events in this quadrennial competition among teams from the Western Hemisphere are show jumping, dressage, and three-day eventing. Shortened to Pan Am Games.

panel
One of the two padded pieces under the cantle of a saddle that rest against the horse's back.

papers
Common term for a registration certificate.

parade
A Western horse show division in which horses are judged at the walk, jog, and lope. The degree of eye-catching animation is taken into consideration, as well as the ornate (often

silver mounted) bridle, breastplate, and saddle they wear.

pari-mutuel
The predominant method of wagering, in which all money bet is divided among holders of winning tickets (after governmental and/or racing agencies deduct their share). From the French *parier mutuel*, meaning "mutual stake" or "betting among ourselves."

park gait
In pleasure driving, a stylishly elegant medium trot.

parlay
In racing, a wager in which the winnings from a preceding race are reinvested.

parrot mouth
The conformation fault of an overshot upper jaw.

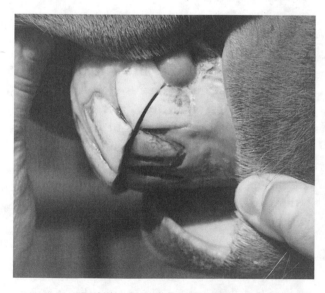

Side view of parrot mouth

(© RICHARD KLIMESH)

pas de deux (PAH-de-DUH)
A dressage exhibition or test in which two riders simultaneously perform a pattern that offers a "mirror image" of each other's movements and transitions. From the French, for "dance for two."

Paso Fino
The breed of laterally-gaited horse that developed in the Caribbean from horses brought to Santo Domingo on Columbus's second voyage. Standing about 14 hands high with fine features that reflect their Arab and Barb forebears, the Paso Fino is characterized by the *paso*, the brilliant yet comfortable four-beat lateral gait (in effect, a broken pace). As distinguished from the Peruvian Paso, the Paso Fino is somewhat smaller with a somewhat shorter stride. Paso Finos are used as show horses and as pleasure mounts.

Paso llano
See Peruvian Paso.

passage (pah-SAHZ)
In dressage, a highly collected trot in which the horse appears to be floating across the ground.

pastern
The portion of the lower leg between the fetlock and the foot. *Cf.* hoof.

past performances
(1) in racing, published information that gives complete details on a horse's previous races and workouts for handicapping purposes;
(2) in horse showing, the record of a horse's points and awards.

patrol judge
In racing, an official who stands on an elevated platform and observes the running of the race in order to report possible infractions to the stewards.

peacock stirrup
See quick release stirrup.

peel
Of cutting cattle, to move single file around the cutting horse and back to the rest of the herd.

Pegasus
In Greek mythology, the winged horse tamed by Perseus when he rescued Andromeda from the Minotaur.

pelham
A bit that combines the effects of a curb and a snaffle.

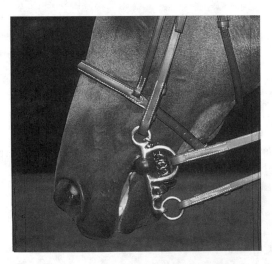

Pelham bit
(© MILLER HARNESS COMPANY L. L. C.)

pelham converter
Two straps, one on each side of a pelham bit, that connects the curb and snaffle bits and enables the rider to use one rein instead of the two normally required when using a pelham (one rein is less likely to slip between the rider's fingers).

penalty
In polo, the result of a foul. Penalties range from automatic goals to defended or undefended shots at various distances from the opposing team's goal.

penning
See team penning.

pentathlon
A five-phase competition that includes show jumping (the other phases are running, pistol shooting, fencing, and swimming). The event replicates the skills once needed to deliver a military message.

Percheron
A draft breed, originating in the La Perche region of northern France. Infusions of Arabian and Barb blood gave the Percheron the most refined features of all the draft breeds. Predominantly colored from light to very dark gray, Percherons have prominent withers, sloping shoulders, and short powerful legs. The largest horse on record was a Percheron that measured twenty-one hands high and weighed in excess of three thousand pounds.

perfecta
In racing, a type of wager in which the bettor must select the first two horses without stipu-

Percheron

(© PERCHERON HORSE
ASSOCIATION OF AMERICA)

Peruvian Paso

(© DEBBIE PYE)

lating the order in which they will finish. *See* exacta.

perfect course (PC)
The result of a show jumping class in which the number of horses in the jump-off round equals the number of prize ribbons being offered in that class.

Peruvian Paso
The breed of laterally-gaited horse that developed in Peru from horses brought by Spanish explorers and colonists. Standing between 14 and 15.2 hands, the Peruvian Paso is slightly larger than its Paso Fino cousins. It moves at two distinctive gaits: the *Paso llano* having an evenly-spaced four-beat cadence; and the *sobreandano*, a faster and slightly more lateral movement. Peruvian Pasos are enjoyed as show horses and for pleasure riding.

pesade
A levade of less than forty-five degrees.

phaeton
In driving, a light four-wheeled carriage with one or two seats that face forward. Phaetons often have a high back and are fancifully and ornately decorated. The name comes from the Greek mythological figure, the son of Apollo, who drove the chariot of the sun so close to Earth that Zeus was obliged to strike down Phaeton with a thunderbolt to prevent the planet from catching fire.

125

photo finish
In racing, the end of a race in which two or more horses finish in such a close order that only a high-speed photograph can show the exact order. Photos can be used to determine not only the winner, but the horse that finished second or third.

piaffe (pee-AFF)
A highly collected trot in place. Found in upper-level dressage tests and also performed by haute école exhibitions, the piaffe requires the highest degree of impulsion and collection. The word is from the French, "to paw the ground in annoyance."

pick out
(1) To use a hoof pick to clean a horse's feet;
(2) To clean a stall of clumps of manure and urine-soaked bedding.

piebald
A pinto or Paint coat consisting of patches of black and white. *Cf.* skewbald.

pigeon-toed
A conformation defect in which the toes of both forelegs angle in toward each other and affect the horse's stride.

pig-eyed
A conformation fault in which unattractively tiny round eyes are set too close together.

piggin' string
A length of rope used by calf ropers to tie the calf's legs together.

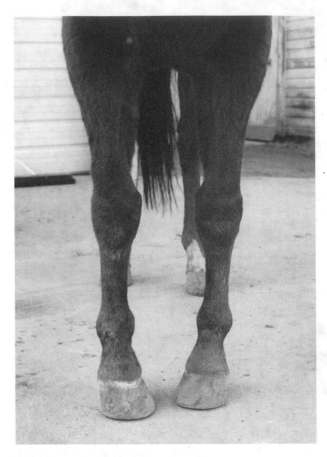

Pigeon-toed horse
(© RICHARD KLIMESH)

pillion
The style of riding, most often found in Spanish folkloric events, in which the woman sits on the horse's rump behind the saddle and holds onto the male rider's waist.

pin firing
The technique of applying heat to a leg with hot needles, done to increase blood flow and thus promote healing. Thanks to more modern methods of increasing blood flow (by means of stimulating medications), the procedure is now rarely done.

pinhook
In racing, to buy a young, usually unraced horse with the purpose of trying to resell the animal at a profit.

pink
The color of the prize ribbon awarded for fifth place.

Pink
The familiar name for the scarlet coat worn by foxhunters, commonly believed to be the name of the London tailor who originated the garment. Also known as hunting pink (not capitalized).

pinto
Any horse with a coat of patches of white and another color above its knee. *See* Paint. Although multicolored horses are most closely associated with Western riding, they have been prized over the centuries throughout the world; pintos can be seen in such widely diverse places as Japanese scrolls and the paintings of the seventeenth-century Spanish artist Velasquez. *See* overo; tobiano.

pinworm
A small parasite that infests the intestines and the rectum. A sure symptom of infection is the horse's rubbing its tail against a fence post or another solid object in an attempt to relieve the anal itch. The remedy is to administer deworming medication.

pipe-opener
In racing, a short vigorous gallop intended to clear the horse's lungs.

pirouette
In dressage, a movement in which the horse's forequarters circle around the hindquarters at the canter, the horse pivoting on one of its hind legs.

pivot
In reining work, a ninety degree turn with one stationary hind foot acting as a pivot. The pivot is similar to the form required for a pirouette.

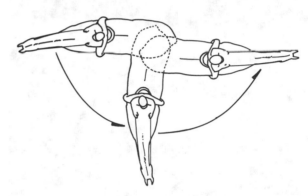

Making two pivots for a 180 degree turn
(© CHERRY HILL 2000)

place
(1) in racing, second position at the finish; (2) to win a ribbon at a horse show.

placing judge
In racing, the official in charge of determining the order of finish. Photo-finish cameras, instant TV replay, and other technological aids assist in making such decisions.

plantar
The ligament below and behind the hock joint.

plate
In racing, a horseshoe most typically made of aluminum. Because of their lightness, plates

are the usual shoes worn by flat and harness horses.

pleasure driving

A horse show class in which horses pull a four-wheel cart and are judged on their movement and manners. Piloted by drivers wearing formal clothing, the horses perform at the walk, park trot, and road trot.

Pleasure driving

(© AMERICAN QUARTER HORSE ASSOCIATION)

Pluvinel de la Baume, Antoine [1555–1620]

French trainer and author, codifier of several haute école movements, including the courbette and capriole. The author of *Instruction du Roi en l'art de monter à Cheval*, a dialogue between him and King Louis XIII, Pluvinal was also the first to introduce pillar work by which a horse was restrained by two posts to encourage haute école collection.

point

(1) the widest part of a body feature, such as point of hip, point of shoulder, or point of hock;

(2) a sharp edge on a cheek tooth, routinely filed away by floating;

(3) the mane, leg, and tail colors or markings when different from the body color.

point-to-point

A hunt race that takes place over a course of obstacles such as hedges, post-and-rails, and other natural obstacles routinely encountered while foxhunting. Entrants in point-to-points are traditionally horses and riders who hunt with the foxhunt that sponsors the race.

pole

(1) in jumping, to rap the hind legs with a bamboo pole when the horse is in the air. Considered illegal by most governing bodies, poling discourages a horse from hitting subsequent fences;

(2) in racing, any of the markers around a track that indicate distances from the finish line, such as the quarter pole or mile pole.

pole bending

A timed Western horse show event in which a horse and rider team weaves between six poles in a slalomlike pattern. The pattern begins with a gallop to the pole farthest from the start/finish line, circles around that pole and slaloming through the others, then slaloming up the poles, rounding the last one and galloping across the start/finish line.

pole position

In racing, the starting-gate position of the horse closest to the inside rail.

Pole bending

(© WYATT MCSPADDEN/AMERICAN
QUARTER HORSE ASSOCIATION)

poll

The highest portion of a horse's head, behind its ears.

poll evil

A bacterial infection of the bursa in the poll area. The symptoms are swelling and drainage of the infection. Antibiotics are the treatment.

polo

A mounted sport in which two opposing teams attempt, with long-handled mallets, to drive a ball between the other team's goal posts (the expression "hockey on horseback" helps to explain the object). Teams consist of four players in outdoor polo and three players in arena, or indoor, polo. Originating in Asia (*polo* is a Tibetan word for "ball"), the sport was introduced to Europe by British cavalrymen who learned to play in India during the nineteenth century. An American newspaperman and sportsman, James Gordon Bennett, brought polo to the United States in 1876. The so-called golden age of American polo took place during the 1920s and 1930s when large crowds lined polo fields to watch professionals, amateurs, and celebrities play. The button-down-collar shirt was devised to keep collar ends out of the eyes of polo players, while the familiar short-sleeve collarless polo shirt relieved players from similar upper-body restraint and distractions.

polo wrap

A type of bandage that extends from the fetlock almost up to the knee. It provides support as well as protecting against the impact of polo balls.

pommel

The elevated front part of an English or Western saddle.

pony

(1) A species of equine that measures no higher than 14.2 hands. A common misunderstanding is that ponies are small horses; they are not—they are separate species. Show ponies are divided into three categories: large, measuring between 13.2 and 14.2 hands; medium, between 12.2 and 13.2; and small, under 12.2. Ponies compete against others of the same category;
(2) A horse of any size used in polo;
(3) As a verb, to lead another horse from horseback.

Pony Club

An educational and recreational equestrian organization for young people under the age of twenty-one. Stressing theoretical and practical knowledge of riding and horse care, the U.S. Pony Club was modeled after the British version and incorporated in 1954. Local chapters are often sponsored by foxhunts. Every Pony Club member is tested and rated at levels that range from D, the most elementary, up to A, which is so demanding that only a few dozen youngsters annually qualify for this level.

Pony of the Americas

A breed of American pony distinguished by its Appaloosa markings, striped hooves, and mottled muzzle. The breed originated in 1956 when an Appaloosa mare was bred to a Shetland pony stallion. The result, named Black Hand, was a miniature Appaloosa, and the new breed's foundation sire.

Ponies of the Americas are used for riding, especially the Western variety.

pony-strided

Of a horse, having a short stride.

pony trekking

Sightseeing on horseback. The phrase—and the concept—is used primarily in Britain, Ireland, and other Western European countries where vacationers ride ponies and horses for full- or half-day escorted outings.

port

The arched portion of the mouthpiece of a curb, Pelham, Kimberwicke, and similar bits. The port acts against the roof of the horse's mouth, causing the animal to flex its head as well as to shift its weight back to its hindquarter as an aid in slowing or halting.

post

(1) to rise out of and sink back into the saddle at the trot in order to make the gait more comfortable for the rider. English-style riders routinely post, as do Western riders when their horses are doing the long trot. The word is derived from *postillion*, the rider who sat on one of a team of coach horses to assist the driver in controlling the horses. *See* diagonal;

(2) in racing, the starting line.

Rider in the rise portion of the post

(© RICHARD KLIMESH)

post entry
A horse whose owner or trainer has been able to enter the animal in a race or other competition right before the competition begins.

posting trot
A trot to which the rider posts (which see), as distinguished from a sitting trot. Also called a rising trot.

post-legged
A conformation fault marked by overly straight angulation between the gaskin and cannon, with a correspondingly straight hock joint.

post parade
The prerace procession of horses in front of the grandstand. The parade gives spectators the chance to see the horses in motion.

post position
In racing, the order of horses in the starting gate, indicated by numbers that begin with the stall closest to the rail. Post positions are assigned by the racing secretary, who draws

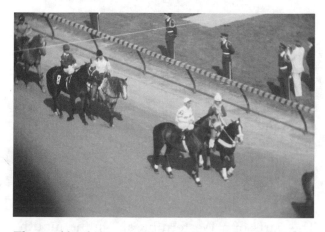
Thoroughbreds in a Kentucky Derby post parade

them randomly by pulling numbered pills out of a box.

post time
In racing, the time when a race is scheduled to begin and when no further wagering is permitted.

Potomac Horse Fever
A debilitating viral infection first identified in the mid-Atlantic states but now found elsewhere in the United States. The cause has not yet been determined. Symptoms include high fever and very loose bowels, often accompanied by laminitis. Treatment is administering fluids and electrolytes, antibiotics, and anti-inflammatory medicine for the laminitis.

power and speed
A show jumping class in which the horse's ability to jump high and then fast are tested. A horse that faultlessly jumps the higher and wider fences of the first part of the course goes on to slightly lower fences where the time to complete that part of the course becomes a determining factor.

prairie grass
A variety of hay grass.

Preakness
The second race of the Triple Crown, held the third Saturday in May at Pimlico Racetrack in Baltimore, Maryland. The race is held at a distance of a mile and three eighths.

preference list
In racing, a system in which horses with the longest time since their last race or chance to

race are given greater consideration to be accepted for the next race for which they qualify.

Preliminary
The combined training level between Training and Intermediate.

prepurchase exam
An assessment by a veterinarian prior to the sale of a horse, usually conducted by the vet chosen by the prospective buyer. The sale is almost always contingent upon the exam.

presentation
In driving, a phase of a combined driving event or a separate event in which entries are judged on the appearance of the horse(s), vehicle, driver, and (if any) grooms.

Prince of Wales spur
The English-style spur that has a thin, curved knob end. Named after the future Edward VII.

produce
The offspring of a mare. The offspring of a stallion is known as his get.

program
A publication that lists entries and other information about the event's participants and competitions. Racing programs may also list the morning line odds.

propping
Seeming to push back with the front legs in what appears to be a momentary hesitation. It is usually caused by being startled or a reluctance to continue moving forward.

protest
In racing, a written complaint against any horse that has started in a race, to be made to the stewards within forty-eight hours after the race was run. An example of a protest may involve the discovery that a certain horse was ineligible for the race in which it ran.

public trainer
In racing, a trainer whose services are available to horse owners in general and who trains the horses of more than one owner. The opposite is a private trainer, who works for only one racing stable.

pull
To shorten a mane or tail by yanking out the longest hairs until the mane or tail reaches the desired length. Pulling manes and tails gives them a more natural look than trimming the ends of the hair. *Cf.* bobtailed, hog, and roach.

pulley rein
An emergency-brake stopping technique in which the rider braces one hand against the horse's withers while pulling the other rein back and up with the other hand. The method gives the rider the greatest leverage, which is useful when trying to deal with a horse that has bolted.

purchase
The parts of a Western bit above the mouthpiece. *See also* shank.

purple
The color of the prize ribbon awarded for seventh place.

purse
The prize monies offered in a competition. In racing, purses generally consist of nomination, sustaining or entry fees, and any added money such as a sponsor's contribution.

put down
To euthanize.

Andalusian

American Saddlebreds

Appaloosa

A palomino Arabian under Western tack

Bank obstacle

Belgian

Chincoteague ponies

Jumping a coop

Driving a four-in-hand

Dressage

Friesian

Icelandic horse

Hunters and foxhounds

Percherons

Calf roping

Drop fence

Polo

Standardbred

Oldenberg

Trakehner obstacle

Water obstacle

Point-to-point race

Morgan

quadrille

A dressage exhibition in which horses and riders execute *haute école* movements choreographed into dance-like routines and performed to musical accompaniment. Although the word suggests that four horses take part, which was indeed the original concept, quadrilles now consist of four, eight or 12. Popular at European courts during the sixteenth to the eighteenth centuries; quadrilles are now most frequently seen as part of performances by the Spanish Riding School and the Cadre Noire.

qualify

To become eligible for further competition, such as end-of-year horse show events, by winning a certain number of points or events.

quarter crack

A crack in the quarter section of the hoof (the portion between the heel and the toe) extending downward from the coronet toward the sole. The most common cause is dryness of the hoof. A bar shoe will stabilize a small crack, which will then be allowed to heal by growing out. Otherwise, the crack must be filled in with a synthetic substance before the

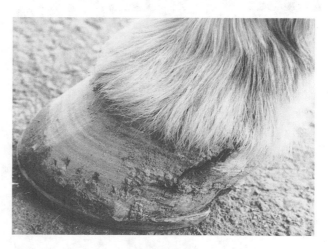

Quarter crack

(© RICHARD KLIMESH)

bar shoe is attached. Also known as sand crack.

Quarter Horse
See American Quarter Horse.

quick release stirrup
An English-style stirrup having its tread held in place by a strong rubber band. The rubber band releases if and when the rider falls to prevent the rider's foot from becoming caught in the stirrup (and the rider being dragged). Also known as a peacock stirrup or a safety stirrup.

quit
In cutting, to stop working a cow, done when, in the rider's estimation, further working would not gain any more points. If time permits, the rider may then ask the horse to cut and work another cow.

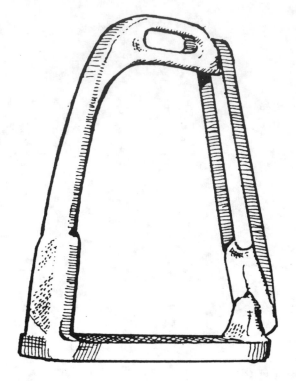

Quick release stirrup

rabbit
In racing, a horse that is sent to the lead to establish a fast pace. The strategy is to tire out other horses so that a horse that is linked with the rabbit in the betting pool can come from behind and win.

racing commission (often known as racing board)
A government-appointed body in charge of regulating and supervising the conduct of racing in a state or province.

racing secretary
In racing, the track official who is responsible for establishing the conditions of races and other general administrative duties.

rack
A rapid lateral gait in which the horse's feet hit the ground individually, usually in a circular pattern (viz., left hind, left fore, right fore, right hind). The predisposition to rack is natural to American Saddlebreds, which when shown at the rack and slow gait in addition to the walk, trot, and canter, are known as five-gaited horses. Other breeds that perform the gait include the Racking Horse and Mountain Horse. *See* slow gait.

rail
(1) The inner barrier around a race track;
(2) In jumping, one of the horizontal wooden poles of which some fences are constructed.

rangy
A slang term for having an easy and loose movement at all gaits.

rank
Difficult to control.

ratcatcher
(1) in foxhunting, informal clothes (e.g., brown boots and tweed coats) worn during the cubbing season. The word refers to the informal style of garments worn by men whose job was to trap rodents;
(2) a woman's collarless riding shirt. Worn with a detachable choker collar, ratcatcher shirts are appropriate for foxhunting and hunter-seat horse showing.

rate
(1) in working cow horse and roping classes, the ability of a horse to maintain relative speed and position on a cow by speeding up or slowing down as necessary, as in "that horse rated his cow just right";
(2) in racing, to encourage a horse to settle down and run in a relaxed fashion.

rating
In polo, the number of goals that a player would theoretically score in a game. Ratings are determined by the U.S. Polo Association. In all but the most informal matches, the ratings for all players on a team are totaled, and, to insure fairness, the lower-rated team begins the match with a score equal to the difference between the two totals. Also known as handicap.

reach
Of a jumping horse, to unfold and then extend the forelegs in order to clear the fence, usually the result of having left the ground too far away from the obstacle.

rearing
The dangerous habit of standing up on the hind legs. Not only is the rider likely to fall off, but the horse is likely to lose its balance and fall over backward.

red
The color of the prize ribbon awarded for second place.

red dun
A form of dun with a yellowish or tan-colored body color and a mane and tail that are red or reddish, flaxen, white, or mixed. The horse also has a red or reddish dorsal stripe and, usually, red or reddish zebra stripes on legs and a transverse stripe over the withers.

red roan
A bay coat with white hairs that give the coat a reddish tinge. A red roan can have a red, black, or flaxen mane and/or tail.

reed canary grass
A hay grass.

refusal
In jumping, a failure to make an attempt to jump. A first refusal is scored as three faults, a second as another six faults, and a third refusal results in elimination.

registration certificate
A document issued by a registry that certifies a horse is duly enrolled. The document includes the birthdate and all identification markings of the animal, registration number, owner, and breeder.

reining
A Western horse show class in which horses are judged on their ability to execute a prearranged pattern of such maneuvers as run-

American Quarter Horse executing a reining pattern
(© D.R. STOECKLEIN / AMERICAN
QUARTER HORSE ASSOCIATION)

downs, sliding stops, rollbacks, circles, and spins. Scoring is done on the basis of seventy as an average ride, with full or half points added or deducted for the way in which the horse performs each of the pattern's movements.

related distance
In jumping, a series of two or more fences of which the measurements between them are counted in terms of a set number of horses' strides. Although there is no hard and fast rule about when related distances end, the widely accepted limit is beyond eight or ten strides.

reins
The straps from the bridle to the rider's hands. Although most reins are made of leather, other materials include canvas and cotton rope. Braided leather or rubber covering helps prevent slipping through the rider's fingers in wet weather. *See also* mecate; romal.

release
In jumping, the manner in which the rider's hands are carried or placed so they do not restrict the horse's head and neck from the take-off to landing. *See* crest release; out-of-hand release.

remount
An obsolete term for any horse used for military purposes. The word is based on the cavalry's need for a great many horses to serve as fresh mounts.

remuda (ruh-MYOOD-uh)
A Western term for a herd from which horses that will be used for the day's work are drawn; from the Spanish for "change [of horses]".

renvers (RON-vair)
In dressage, a two-track oblique movement in which the horse's forelegs stay on an inner track and his hind legs on an outer track. *See* travers.

reserve
Second place in the championship award standings. The horse or rider is known as the reserve champion and wins a tricolor ribbon of yellow, red, and white.

resistance-free training
The technique of getting a horse to accept being handled, tacked, and ridden that emphasizes patience and an understanding of the equine mind instead of relying on force. *See also* horse gentler.

restricted stakes
In racing, a stakes race limited to horses that meet certain criteria, such as having been bred

in a particular state or purchased through or consigned to a particular sale.

return
A clause in a breeding contract that provides that mares that do not become pregnant may be bred again at no cost.

Rhinelander
A German Warmblood breed that was developed in the Rhineland, Westphalia, and Saxony regions. Like other central European Warmbloods, Rhinelanders stand approximately 16.2 hands, have good bone and muscle, and are used in dressage and show jumping.

rhinopneumonitis
A contagious upper-respiratory condition with symptoms that include weakness, fever, dry cough, and a nasal discharge. Serious neurological complications may develop, too. A vaccine offers short-term immunity. Otherwise, administering antibiotics and fluids is the treatment.

ribbon
The traditional rosette prize awarded in horse shows. The ribbon's color designates the order of finish: blue for first place, red for second, yellow for third, white for fourth, pink for fifth, green for sixth, purple for seventh, and brown for eighth. In addition, the tricolor ribbon awarded to the high-point champion of a division is a combination of blue, red, and white; the ribbon for reserve champion is red, yellow, and white.

ridden out
In racing, to finish the race under mild urging, usually with a limited use of the whip.

ride and tie
A competition in which teams composed of two humans and one horse cover a distance of between twenty-five and forty miles. One person rides the horse as far as he or she thinks the other person can run, then dismounts and ties the horse to a tree or another object and continues along the course on foot. The second person reaches the horse and rides past the first person. This leapfrog continues until the team all cross the finish line. The team that completes the course in the fastest time is the winner.

ride-off
See test.

riding off
In polo, a defensive maneuver in which a player moves his pony's shoulder against an opposing pony's shoulder so the first animal can push the opponent away from the line of the ball.

rimfire
The term that describes the double rigging of a Western saddle that is so rigged.

ringbone
Arthritis of the joints caused by new bone growth around the pastern joint (high ringbone) or around the coffin joint (low ringbone). The growth is precipitated by sudden or constant strain to the foot. Symptoms include heat, swelling, and eventual lameness. If and when corrective shoeing and anti-inflammatory medication can no longer help, surgery may be indicated.

ringmaster
The horse show official who announces the start of each class, customarily by sounding a

coach horn. Dressed in a coachman's scarlet coat, the ringmaster also helps in award presentation.

rising
Approaching in age. A horse that is "rising eight" is almost eight years old.

rising trot
The posting trot.

RNPA
In polo, a mallet head having a rounded midsection and tapered flat ends. The initials stand for Royal Naval Polo Association.

roach
(1) curved or rounded, as a roached back of a horse or rider;
(2) to trim a mane so short that the hairs stand up, done for appearance, ease of care, and to keep the mane out of the way of the rider.

road gait
In pleasure driving, an extended trot that is faster than the park gait.

roads and tracks
One of the phases of the speed and endurance part of a three-day event. Horses and riders must cover a course without jumps within a certain time, usually at a brisk trot. Roads and tracks is essentially a warm-up effort.

Roadster Pony
A horse show class in which Hackneys ponies pull road wagons or sulky bikes and are judged on their animated walk and trot.

road wagon
A light four-wheeled vehicle used in Roadster Pony classes.

roaring
A deep throaty noise made during exercise. It is caused by a partial paralysis of the larynx that surgery is often able to correct.

rockgrinder
A Western spur with eighteen tines on its rowel.

Rocky Mountain Horse
The American breed descended from horses brought to America by Spanish explorers and colonists and characterized by a natural four-beat ambling gait in which all four feet are heard striking the ground individually. Standing 14-2 to 16 hands, with a solid coat (most often a light chocolate brown) and flaxen mane and tail, the Rocky Mountain Horse breed is traced back to Old Tobe, a prepotent stallion owned by Sam Tuttle of Kentucky. Rocky Mountain Horses are used as pleasure mounts and in competitive trail and endurance riding.

rodeo
A Western competition composed of such events as calf roping, bareback and saddle bronc riding, bull riding, steer wrestling, and barrel racing. The sport developed from informal competitions in which cowboys vied to see who was the best rider or owned the best ranch horse, with wagering backing up the boasts. The 1800s saw the first formal rodeos with entry fees and admission charges making up the prize money. There are now thousands of rodeos in the United States and

Canada, together with considerable TV coverage.

rogue
Willfully bad tempered; also, roguey.

rollback
In reining, a movement in which the horse halts, turns 180 degrees by pivoting on the inside hind leg, and then lopes off.

roller
See anticast roller.

rollers
Small rotating devices on the mouthpiece of a bit. They encourage a horse to salivate, which in turn makes the bit more palatable and the horse more responsive to the bit.

Romal

(© CHERRY HILL)

Bit with rollers

(© MILLER HARNESS COMPANY L. L. C.)

romal(roh-MAHL)
(1) A type of rein in which the straps coming from the bit join into one rein at the point where the rider holds them;
(2) The Western style of riding in which the rider uses such a rein.

roman nose
Of a horse, a face with a convex, or bulging, profile.

roping
See calf roping; team roping.

rose gray
The body color composed of a mixture of chestnut and white hairs.

142

rosinback
The slang term for a draft horse that is used as a vaulting horse in the circus. Dusting a horse's back with rosin reduces the chance of the acrobat's feet slipping.

rough board
An accommodations arrangement in which the horse is fed and watered and its stall mucked out. All other chores, such as grooming and exercise, are the responsibility of the horse's owner. *Cf.* full board.

roundup
Gathering pastured cattle or horses into a large group preparatory to moving the herd to another location.

rowel
The pointed wheel of a spur. A roweled spur is a traditional Western accessory. Some dressage spurs have tiny rowels. The length, shape (especially whether the end is sharp or blunt), and number of rowels determine the spur's severity.

rub
In jumping, contact by a horse's foot or leg against the top of a fence that is not hard enough to knock the fence down; also called a touch or tick.

rub on
To groom, as in "I've rubbed on that horse for a year now."

rug
An old British term for a horse blanket.

run-down
(1) In reining, a pattern movement in which the horse lopes or gallops from one end of the arena to the other. The movement begins with rapid acceleration and usually ends with a sliding stop;
(2) A type of protective bandage worn to protect the ankles against abrasions.

running walk
A half-walk/half-trot gait natural to Tennessee Walking Horses and certain other gaited breeds.

run out
In jumping, a refusal that takes the form of evading the fence by passing to one side.

rye
A cereal used as feed.

rye grass
A hay grass also used as straw.

S

saddle

(1) the piece of tack in which a rider sits. The two major classifications are the Western, or stock saddle, with its high pommel and cantle designed for comfort and function while doing ranch work, and the English saddle,

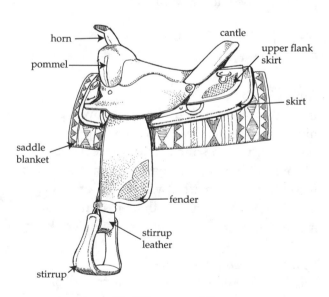

The Western saddle

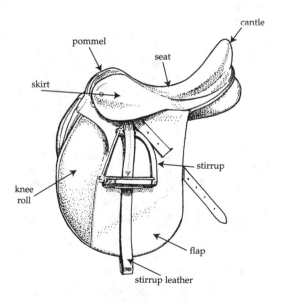

The English saddle

flatter and thinner to allow greater contact between the rider's seat and legs and the horse. Within the Western category are saddles designed for such activities as roping, reining, and barrel racing, along with ones with ornate silver ornamentation for parade use. English saddles include the forward-seat variety for jumping, an even flatter dressage and gaited-horse type, and others for distance riding, racing, sidesaddle riding, and polo;

(2) in driving, the piece of harness on the back of the horse to which the terrets are attached.

Saddlebred
See American Saddlebred.

saddle mark
A marking of white hairs on the part of the back where the saddle goes.

saddle-seat equitation
The English-style technique used to ride American Saddlebreds, Tennessee Walking Horses,

Saddle-seat equitation

and other gaited horses. The rider's position is characterized by straight legs held away from the horse's sides and hands held relatively high.

saddle soap
A glycerin-based soap used to clean and condition leather.

saddle sore
A raw sore on the back caused by the rubbing of a badly fitted saddle or saddle blanket or pad. Treatment includes cleaning and dressing the wound (and draining any trapped pus or blood) followed by rest until the wound has healed.

safety stirrup
See quick release stirrup.

sand colic
Colic that results when a horse's feed is placed on sandy ground or when the animal develops the bad habit of eating sand.

sand crack
See quarter crack.

sandwich box
In foxhunting and in horse show appointments classes, the leather case strapped to the saddle in which sandwiches are carried. Traditionally, the fare is ham or another plain meat between bread of which the crusts have been removed (on the theory that crustless sandwiches are less likely to cause choking).

Santini, Piero [1881–1960]
Italian horseman and author, a friend of Federico Caprilli and an early advocate of Caprilli's forward-seat riding.

savage
To attack another horse or another living creature (including a human).

school
To train a horse. A schooling class at a horse show or a schooling show itself is intended to be a young horse's initial exposure to competition.

schooling ring
The warm-up area at a horse show. Known in other countries as the collecting ring.

school movements (or figures)
Exercises and movements associated with classical horsemanship, such as the shoulder-in, renvers, passage, and piaffe; also known as manège movements.

sclera
The visible white outer membrane of the eye, best known among horsemen as the human-eye feature of the Appaloosa.

Scotch
Of a calf-roping horse, to halt before being given the cue to do so; also called set up.

Scotch spire
In driving, the tall decorative projection on the harness collar. Chiefly worn on the show or exhibition harness of draft horses.

Scout
The pinto ridden by Tonto, sidekick of the Lone Ranger, in the Lone Ranger movies and television series.

scratch
To withdraw an entered horse from a race or horse show. In racing, scratch time is generally twenty-four hours before race day, although for stakes races, horses can be scratched up to fifteen minutes before post time. In most instances, horse show entries can be scratched the day of the competition only under instructions from or with the approval of a veterinarian.

scurf (or scarf)
A dermatological condition marked by scaly or encrusted skin. Shampooing with tar-based or other types of medicated soap is the treatment.

seat
(1) The portion of a saddle that accommodates the rider's buttocks;
(2) A secure position in the saddle, as in the expression "she has a good seat";
(3) A specific style of riding, such as Western stock seat and English hunt seat or saddle seat.

second-year green
A show hunter in its second year of competition at a recognized horse show. Fences in this division are set at three feet six inches. Following a horse's second-year green year, it becomes an open hunter.

see a distance
See distance.

seedy toe
A separation of the wall of the hoof from the laminae.

segunda
A snaffle bit with a raised horseshoe-shaped center that acts in the manner of a port.

self-carriage
The ability of a horse to move in a light and balanced fashion without the assistance or support of the rider's reins.

Selle Français
The sport horse of France, first bred in Normandy in the nineteenth century by crossing Thoroughbreds with native Warmblood stock. The result was a horse that resembles the Thoroughbred in size and quality, with an athleticism that lends itself to show jumping in particular. The formal name, *le cheval de selle français*, translates as "French saddle horse."

senior
(1) A horse above the age of five;
(2) A person eighteen years or older. Below eighteen, a rider, driver or handler is a junior.

serpentine
A movement called for in several dressage and other riding tests that is composed of a series of linked S-shaped changes of direction across an arena.

sesamoid (SES-a-moid)
One of two small bones above and at the back of the fetlock joint. Sesamoiditis is an inflammation of these bones that comes from a strain of the ligaments that hold the bones in place. The treatment is support bandages or a cast, anti-inflammation medication, and rest.

set
In jumping, to design or build a course of obstacles, as in the sentence "The course designer set a challenging course for the Grand Prix."

set down
In racing, to suspend or to be suspended from riding or training, typically after a jockey has been found guilty of committing a foul or a trainer for an infraction of the rules of racing.

settle
(1) to allow a horse to relax at the halt;
(2) to allow a herd of cattle to become accustomed to the arena.

set up
See Scotch.

sex allowance
The practice of allowing fillies and mares to carry less weight when racing against male horses.

shadbelly
A formal riding coat with a waist-length front and long tails. Worn over a lighter colored vest and shirt, a shadbelly is traditional in upper-level dressage tests and important hunter

Dressage rider wearing a formal riding coat, or shadbelly.
(© ED CAMELLI)

classes. (The word was inspired by the pale stomach of the shad fish.)

shadow roll
In racing, a piece of sheepskin placed across a horse's nose to block the sight of distracting shadows on the ground.

shank
(1) the long leverlike pieces of a curb or pelham bit to which the reins are attached. The longer the shank, the greater the bit's leverage action; (2) any part of a Western bit below the mouthpiece;

American Quarter Horse wearing a shadow roll and blinkers

(3) The rope or strap by which a haltered horse is led. Many shanks have a section of chain above a leather strap; the chain can be placed across the horse's muzzle for greater control. Also known as the lead shank.

shape
In cutting, to move the herd at the beginning of the round so that the most cutable cows stay to the front and the least desirable ones rejoin the main herd at the back fence. Shaping is the job of the turnback riders.

shavings
Small thin strips of wood used as stall bedding. In many parts of the country, shavings are as accessible and less expensive than straw bedding.

sheath
The tube of skin that surrounds the penis. For sanitary reasons, the sheath must be periodically cleaned.

shedding blade
A grooming tool with an oval, serrated metal blade, used to remove loose hair and dirt.

shed row
In racing, the backstretch area of stables that have outside walkways below an overhanging roof.

sheet
A light blanket, usually made of canvas, cotton, or nylon, and worn by horses when a wool or quilted blanket would be too warm.

Shetland
A breed of pony native to the Shetland Islands of northern Scotland. Its origins are uncertain,

Shetland Pony

although speculations include Spanish horses and Icelandic ponies that grew small because of the region's sparse vegetation. Shetlands are tiny, measuring ten to twelve hands, with shaggy coats and short legs. Remarkably strong for their diminutive size, they are used for riding and for pulling wagons.

shipping boots
Protective padded coverings for the lower legs, worn during van or trailer trips.

Shire
The largest of the draft breeds, originating in the north of England. Because of its size—it

Shire

can reach eighteen hands and weigh more than a ton—the breed is thought to have the closest connection to the Flemish War Horse. Shires have prominent eyes, a broad forehead, a relatively long neck, and muscular shoulders and hindquarters. Like other draft breeds, they are used for hauling and other transportation work.

shooting brake
In driving, a four-wheeled vehicle with one or more rows of seats that can be folded or removed to make room for luggage, especially for sporting gear.

shoulder
The portion of the body between the neck and barrel, to which the forelegs are attached.

shoulder-in
A school movement in which the horse moves forward with its forequarters bent toward the inside of the arena. When done properly, the inside hind foot and the outside forefoot travel on the same track.

show
In racing, to finish in third place.

showmanship
A Western horse show class for youth and amateur exhibitors in which how well the exhibitors present their halter horses is judged (the quality of the animals is not taken into consideration).

sickle-hocked
A conformation fault in which the hind hocks and lower legs curve under the body.

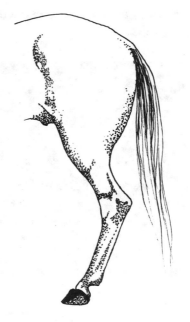

Sickle hock

(© CHRISTINA BERUBE)

sidebone
A hardening of the cartilage occurring most usually in the forefeet. Although sidebone will not of itself cause lameness, it can lead to corns and cracked heels. Thinning the hoof to relieve pressure across the heels, together with corrective shoeing, will help a horse with sidebones.

side-pass
A lateral maneuver in which the horse moves to the side, with no forward or backward motion.

side reins
A training device consisting of a pair of reins that run from either side of the saddle through the bit rings to the rider's hands or, on an unridden horse, from either side of the surcingle to the bit rings or the halter. Side reins influ-

151

ence a horse's head carriage, especially with regard to flexion.

Side reins

(© RICHARD KLIMESH)

Nineteenth-century illustration of a sidesaddle rider

sidesaddle

A style of horsemanship for women in which the rider sits with both legs on the (usually) left side of the saddle. The style originated during the fourteenth century, before which women rode astride. A nineteenth-century invention, the leaping head, is a curved armlike projection over which the rider drapes her right leg for security, especially while jumping. Sidesaddle hunter classes, in which riders wear formal riding habits, are a feature of some English horse shows.

silks

In racing, the distinctive shirt and cap worn by jockeys or drivers to identify the horse's owner or, sometimes, the entry's post position. Silks are registered with the appropriate governing body, such as the Jockey Club for Thoroughbred racing, the U.S. Harness Racing Association for Standardbreds. The word refers to the garments originally having been

made of silk, although they are now made of easy-to-launder synthetics.

Silver

The white horse of the crime-fighting Lone Ranger in the Western movies and television series.

simple change of lead

The change of lead at the canter or lope that goes through the trot. The horse makes the transition down to one or more trotting steps before striking off on the other canter lead. *Cf.* flying change of lead.

single foot

See slow gait.

singles

In driving, a competition for vehicles pulled by one horse. *Cf.* pair; four-in-hand.

sitting trot
A trot to which the rider does not post. *Cf.* posting trot.

skene
In polo, a mallet head that has a flat bottom and both ends tapered at the same angle; designed by Bob Skene, a noted polo player.

skewbald
The coat of a pinto that consists of patches of white and any color other than black. *See* piebald.

skid boots
Protective devices worn on hind-leg pasterns and fetlocks. They are also known as sliding boots because of their protection against the abrasion of sliding stops in reining, roping, and other Western events.

skirt
(1) On a Western saddle, the portion of a saddle under the cantle;
(2) On an English saddle, the flap over the stirrup bars; its purpose is to protect the rider's leg from rubbing against the girth buckle and the stirrup bar.

slip
To lengthen the reins by letting them slide through the fingers.

sloppy
In racing, a track surface marked by abundant surface water. *Cf.* muddy.

slow
In racing, a track surface having damp and clinging footing.

slow gait
A lateral gait in which the horse's feet hit the ground individually, natural to American Saddlebreds and other breeds. It is similar to, but slower than, the rack (which see). Also known as single-foot.

smooch
In racing, the kissing "chirp" sound made by jockeys to encourage horses to run faster.

snaffle
A bit with a straight or jointed mouthpiece and without a port. The snaffle is one of the two major categories of bits (the curb is the other). Working primarily on the corners of the horse's mouth, a snaffle exerts more direct pressure than a curb's leverlike action does. This direct pressure is useful for turning as well as stopping the horse. In general, the snaffle is a milder bit than a curb. *See also* elevator bit, gag snaffle, Kimberwicke, pelham.

snip
A white marking near the nostrils.

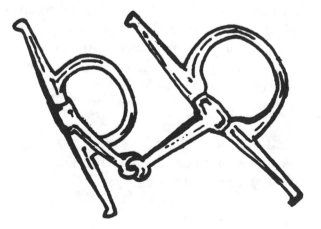

Snaffle bit (full cheek type)

(© CHERRY HILL 2000)

153

Sobreandano
See Peruvian Paso.

sock
A white marking on the cannon, from the coronet halfway to the knee on a foreleg or halfway to the hock on a hind leg.

soft
(1) In racing, a turf surface of deep to heavy footing with substantial moisture;
(2) Of a rider's hands, sensitive to the horse's mouth;
(3) Of a horse's mouth, sensitive to the bit and the rider's hands; *cf.* hard.

sole
The bottom or undersection of the foot, surrounded by the hoof.

sophomore
(1) A three-year-old racehorse;
(2) A horse in its second season of competition.

sorrel
A reddish or copper-red body color; the mane and tail are usually the same color as the body, but they may be flaxen. Although often considered a Western term for chestnut, sorrel is a somewhat lighter reddish-brown than chestnut.

sound
In healthy condition. The word usually refers to an absence of lameness.

sour
Of cutting cattle, unresponsive to the horse, caused by overuse.

soybeans
A legume plant used as feed.

spade
A curb bit having a narrow port with a square top (the spade). Two pieces of wire called "keepers" are attached to the bottom of the spade

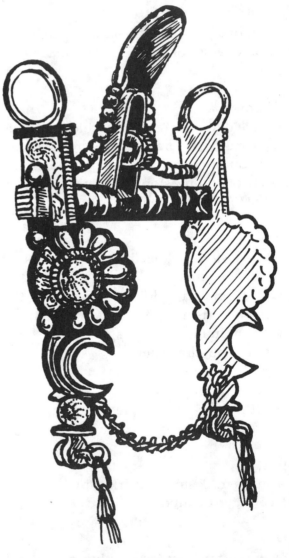

Spade bit

(© CHERRY HILL 2000)

piece and each cheekpiece. The mouthpiece is joined to the cheeks either by a hinge (making the bit a loose-jaw or soft spade) or by welding (a solid-jaw or hard spade). Although the potential for extreme pressure against the roof of the mouth has given the spade bit the reputation as being severe, in the hands of an experienced rider it is no more harsh than any other curb bit.

Spanish Riding School

The establishment in Vienna, Austria, dedicated to the preservation of classical horsemanship. Founded in the seventeenth century with horses imported from Spain (hence the establishment's name), the school moved to its present baroque headquarters in 1735. Its Lipizzaner horses are trained and exhibited by riders, who wear Napoleonic-era uniforms, to the highest standard of haute école horsemanship.

Spanish walk

A classical movement distinguished by well-elevated forelegs. The purported intention was so the animals would not trample the young plants in Spanish vineyards.

spavin

An enlargement of the hock. *See* bog spavin; bone spavin.

speculum

A mechanical apparatus that keeps a horse's mouth open during dental work.

speed and endurance

The second day of a three day event, comprised of the roads and tracks, steeplechase, and cross-country phases. Usually referred to just as the cross-country.

Speed-and-endurance segment of combined training
(© CHERRY HILL)

speed class

In show jumping, the familiar term for a one-round class in which the fastest time determines the winner, with penalty seconds added to the actual time for any knockdowns.

spin

In reining, a maneuver in which the horse makes one or more 360 degree turns while pivoting around an inside hind foot.

Spinning
(© CHERRY HILL)

splay-footed
A conformation fault in which the toes point out and away from each other.

splinter-belly
A horse whose jumping style is to skim across the top of a fence without a noticeable bascule arc.

splints
An inflammation of the ligament that attaches the splint bone to the cannon bone of a front leg. They most often happen following a kick or another blow to the area or from stress due to exertion or faulty conformation. Swelling and heat are the symptoms, as well as an obvious lameness. The treatment includes ice, anti-inflammatory medication, and, if a bony growth develops on the splint bone, surgical removal of the growth.

split reins
Reins with ends that are not joined, a characteristic of Western tack.

sprint
A race under one mile in length.

spurs
Metal devices strapped to the heels of boots to emphasize the rider's leg aids. Western spurs customarily have rowels. Among types of English spurs are the medium-long-necked Prince of Wales, the short-necked Tom Thumb, and the blunt hammerhead.

stable
A structure in which horses live; familiarly called a barn.

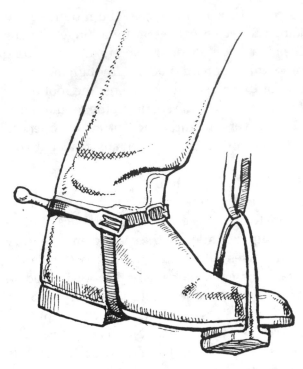

English spur

stable vice
An unwelcome habit such as stall walking or cribbing, often caused by boredom.

stacked
A Western style of pants legs with several accordionlike folds between the knees and cuffs when the wearer is standing. The folds straighten to cover the entire length of the wearer's legs when the person is on horseback.

stakes
(1) In racing, a race for higher-caliber horses in which the owners of entered horses post a nominating and starting fee, which is added to the purse;

(2) The class in a horse show division with the largest amount of prize money.

stakes placed
Finishing second or third in a stakes race.

stakes producer
In racing, a mare that has produced at least one foal that finished first, second, or third in a stakes race.

stakes winner
A horse that has won a stakes race.

stall
A compartment of a stable in which a horse lives. *See* box stall; straight stall.

stall guard
A restraint made of canvas or another fabric that keeps a horse inside a stall when the door has been opened or removed.

stallion
An ungelded male horse of three years or older.

stall walking
A stable vice in which a horse constantly walks back and forth inside its stall. The habit comes from inactivity that leads to boredom.

stamp his get
Of a stallion, to produce offspring that closely resemble their sire.

stand
To offer a stallion for breeding.

Standardbred
The breed most closely associated with harness racing. Although the nominal foundation sire was Messenger, a Thoroughbred imported to the U.S. in the late eighteenth century, the most influential stallion was Hambletonian. Foaled in 1849, he sired more than 1,300 foals, and most Standardbreds can trace their ancestry back to him.

The "standard" in the breed's name comes from the requirement in 1879 that horses had to trot or pace one mile in 1 minute 20 seconds or less in order to be eligible for the American Trotting Registry.

Standardbred harness racing has been a popular pastime at county fairs starting after the Civil War, as well as at harness raceways throughout the world. Horses race as either trotters or pacers (the proclivity for pacing is hereditary and is enhanced through training). Drivers sit in bike-wheeled sulkies, and races begin with the assistance of a mobile starting gate (which see). Most races are at a distance of one mile, which the better horses cover in under 2 minutes; pacers tend to be somewhat faster than trotters.

The most famous race for Standardbreds is the Hambletonian, for three-year-old trotters, held in August at The Meadowlands in New Jersey. Pacing's classic race, also for three-year-olds, is The Little Brown Jug held in September at the Delaware, Ohio, Fairgrounds.

standard
In jumping, the wooden posts that hold the cups in which the rails of a jump rest.

standing bandages
Thick cotton wraps used to prevent swelling and injury during shipping or while the horse is in its stall.

Applying standing bandages

star
A white marking on the forehead.

stargazer
The term for a horse that carries its head in the air.

starter
In racing, the official in charge of overseeing the beginning of a race, especially with regard to making sure the field gets off to a fair start.

starter race
In racing, an allowance or handicap restricted to horses that have run for a specific claiming price.

starting gate
In racing, the multistall apparatus (or in harness racing, the vehicle) from which horses begin a race. *See* mobile starting gate.

state-bred
In racing, a horse bred and/or foaled in one of the United States and which meets the criteria to be eligible to compete in special races or purse supplements.

steady
To slow a horse's speed, often to improve its balance.

steel gray
The body color composed of a mixture of black and white hairs.

steeplechase
(1) a race in which horses jump a course of brush or wooden fences. The name comes from impromptu seventeenth-century races where foxhunters raced across country toward a church steeple, the most visible landmark in the area, and jumping whatever obstacles stood in their way. *See also* hurdle race, point-to-point;

Steeplechase race

(2) the portion of the speed and endurance part of a three-day event that involves a jumping course of hedge obstacles.

step oxer
An oxer of which the elements are set progressively higher. The lowest rail is in the front.

sterm
In foxhunting, a fox hound's hindquarters.

steward
(1) a horse show official who adjudicates alleged rule violations;

Step oxer

(© ED CAMELLI)

(2) in racing, one of the officials who rule on foul claims, institute inquiries, and enforce other regulations.

stick
(1) in jumping, to hesitate in leaving the ground;
(2) a term for a whip or crop.
(3) the familiar term for the device, usually an oversized ruler with a sliding crossbar, with which ponies and horses are measured in height, as in "put a stick to that horse."

stifle
The joint between the thigh and the gaskin, the equivalent of the human hip joint.

stirrup
One of the two metal or wood attachments to the saddle that support the rider's feet. Among the Western varieties are the oxbow and Visalia; the most popular English type is the Fillis.

stirrup bar
The metal device on a saddle that holds the stirrup leathers. A hinge that opens when

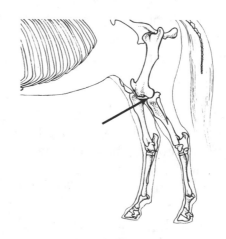

Stifle joint

(© CHRISTINA BERUBE)

pressure is applied is intended to let the stirrup leather slip out so a fallen rider cannot be dragged.

stirrup leathers
The straps from which stirrups are suspended.

stocking
A white marking extending from fetlock to knee or hock.

stock seat
Western-style riding. The word *stock* originally applied to a supply of cattle, and by extension, a ranchman.

stock tie
A knotted white neckcloth worn during the formal foxhunting season and by some upper-level dressage and combined training riders. The ends are pinned to the rider's shirt to keep them from flapping. The garment can serve as an impromptu sling in the event the rider's arm is damaged in a fall.

stone
In racing, a unit of British weight equaling fourteen pounds. The word is used in connection with the amount of weight a horse must carry in a race.

stone bruise
An injury to the sole or frog caused by a pebble or stone. Removing the offending object is the usual remedy, along with rest.

stop
(1) In reining and working cow horse classes, a halt from the gallop in which the horse shifts its weight to its haunches and slides to a com-

Stock tie

(© ED CAMELLI)

plete stop, its hindquarters seeming to "melt" into the ground. Also known as sliding stop; (2) Jumping, the informal term for a refusal.

A reining horse's dramatic sliding stop

(© AMERICAN QUARTER HORSE ASSOCIATION)

straight stall
A rectangular compartment in a stable in which a horse lives. *Cf.* box stall.

strangles
A contagious abscess of the lymph nodes of the neck or jaw. Symptoms are loss of appetite, nasal discharge, and coughing, in addition to swelling of the lymph nodes. Treatment involves draining the nodes and administering antibiotics. Also known as distemper.

strawberry roan
A nickname for a red roan.

stretch
In racing, the straight portion of the track leading to the finish line; also called the home stretch.

stride
The full length of a step at any of the gaits. The size of a stride can be adjusted by collection and extension. *See also* add a stride; leave out a stride.

stringhalt
A muscle condition revealed by the exaggerated involuntary flexing of the hock joint while the horse is moving. Sometimes the hind leg is lifted so high that the animal kicks itself in the belly. Of unknown cause, stringhalt can often be corrected with muscle relaxants or the removal of a section of the affected leg muscle.

strip
A narrow marking extending vertically between the forehead and nostrils.

strongyles (STRONG-jiles)
A parasitic disease transmitted by bloodworms that causes anemia and intestinal tissue damage. A deworming program is both the best prevention and cure.

substance
A complimentary word describing good bone and muscles.

suckling
A foal that receives its nourishment from its mother's milk. When the foal begins to take nourishment on its own, it becomes a weanling.

Suffolk Punch
A breed of draft horse originating in the English county of Suffolk. The foundation sire was Crisp's Horse of Ufford, foaled in 1760. Compact in size and chestnut in color, the Punch stands about sixteen hands and weighs close to one ton when full grown. It is used for agricultural work and for pulling wagons.

sulky
The two-wheel cart used in harness racing. Bicycle or disc wheels support the lightweight metal frame and the driver, who sits with ex-

Standardbred and sulky

tended legs right behind the horse. Light sulkies called bikes are used in some Roadster Pony horse show classes, in which the drivers wear harness racing silks.

The name comes from an old English word having the same root as "sulk" or "brood," suggesting that someone who is pouting would prefer to be alone in a one-person vehicle. Also known as bike.

surcingle
(1) A strap that fastens around the horse's girth to hold a blanket in place;
(2) A strap that fastens around the horses's girth to provide extra security for a racing saddle; also known as an overgirth.

suspensory
The ligament behind the knee or the top of the hind leg cannon bone. Attached to the sesamoid bones, it supports the fetlocks.

swamp fever.
See equine infectious anemia.

swapping leads
Colloquial term for a flying change of lead.

swayback
A distinctly concave backbone, especially behind the withers. A swayback is often, but not always, a sign of age.

Swedish oxer
In jumping, a fence composed of two sets of rails that slope in opposite directions to look like an X when viewed from the front or rear.

Swedish Warmblood
A breed native to Sweden, developed as a military mount by crossing Thoroughbreds,

Swedish oxer

(© ED CAMELLI)

Trakaheners, and Hanoverians with native horses. Strong, compact, and with kind dispositions, Swedish Warmbloods have proven to be outstanding dressage horses.

sweeny
An atrophy of the shoulder muscles caused by damage to the nerves of that area. If anti-inflammatory medication proves inadequate, surgery to repair the muscles is usually indicated.

sweet feed
Grain mixed with molasses or another sweetener. The addition of the sugary ingredient keeps the loose grain together and makes the mixture more palatable, so even the most finicky eater will be more likely to consume its entire ration.

Swift, Sally
See Centered Riding.

synthetic saddle
A saddle made of durable fabric. Lightweight and relatively low cost, it is popularly used in competitive trail riding.

tack
A collective term for saddles, bridles, harness, and other items that horses wear.

tack trunk
A large container in which saddlery and other items for horse and rider are kept; also known as a tack box.

tail bag
A cloth container in which the tail is wrapped to be kept clean.

tail shot
In polo, a stroke in which the player's mallet makes contact with the ball behind the pony's hindquarters.

take
The portion of money wagered that the state and racing commission deduct before the pari-mutuel payoff is computed.

take up
In racing, to restrain a horse sharply to avoid causing or becoming involved in an accident.

tally-ho!
(1) In foxhunting, a shout of encouragement to the hounds when a fox is first sighted. [From Old French, a huntsman's cry];
(2) *Without exclamation point* any mail coach or four-in-hand driving vehicle.

tanbark
Chips of the bark of certain trees once used for tanning leather and then as footing for riding

arenas. The word now metaphorically refers to the horse show ring.

tandem
In driving, a two-horse hitch with one horse in front of the other. *Cf.* pair.

tapadero
A leather cuplike device over the front of some Western stirrups, to protect the rider's feet against thorns and other sharp objects.

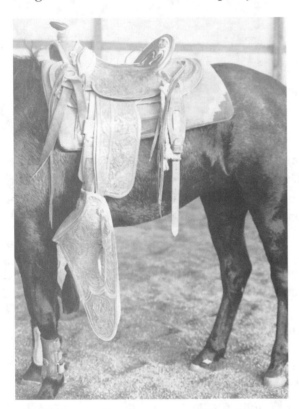

An ornate tapadero

(© CHERRY HILL)

tarpan
A prehistoric wild horse type that ranged from Southern France and Spain eastward to central Russia. The original wild tarpan died out during the late nineteenth century when the horses' natural forest and steppe habitat was destroyed to make room for more people.

The modern tarpan is a genetic recreation of the original wild breed based on genetic material from several European pony breeds, including the Icelandic pony, that had descended from the prehistoric tarpan. Mares from these breeds were then mated to Przewalski's Horse stallions during the 1930s. There are fewer than 200 tarpans today, most of whom live on preserves in Poland.

Standing about 13 hands high, the modern tarpan is dun in color, with a thick thatched mane. The head is large, with massive jaws and thick neck. The hooves are dark and very tough, never requiring shoes.

tattoo
An identification marking of letters and/or numerals placed under a horse's upper lip. Combinations and sequences of letters and numbers can indicate the year the animal was foaled, as well as other data. Racetrack officials examine tattoos before the horses leave the barn area for their race to insure the proper horses will compete on that day.

team penning
A Western event in which teams of three riders remove three specified cows from a herd, then drive them in an enclosure (the pen) at the opposite end of the arena. Riders coordinate their efforts, especially with regard to making sure the cows don't slip back to the herd, by shouts and hand signals. The team that pens the three cows in the fastest time wins.

team roping
A Western event in which two ropers, the header and the heeler, constitute a team that

attempts to rope a calf or steer in the shortest amount of time. As soon as the header has roped the calf's head, the heeler tosses a loop around one of the animal's hind legs. Time is taken when the calf is stretched out. The activity is based on the ranch chore of immobilizing a calf or steer for medical attention. *See* calf roping.

teaser
As used in the breeding process, a male horse that provokes the mare to be bred. Once the mare demonstrates her receptiveness, the teaser is replaced by the breeding stallion.

Technical Delegate (TD)
The official at a dressage, driving, or combined training competition who is responsible for interpreting and enforcing the rules of that sport's governing body.

tempo (Italian for "time");
(1) The speed of footfalls at a gait;
(2) In dressage, the number of strides between flying changes of lead. Two-tempi changes means changing the lead after every two strides.

tendon boots
Leather devices worn on the backs of the ankles of the forelegs to protect against hind feet striking the forefeet.

Tennessee Walking Horse
The American breed of saddle horse noted for its smooth running walk and rocking-chair canter. Developed in the decades before the Civil War as a comfortable mount on which plantation owners could inspect their vast holdings, the Tennessee Walker combined strains of Thor-

Tennessee Walking Horse
(© STUART VESTY/TENNESSEE WALKING
HORSE BREEDERS' & EXHIBITORS' ASSOCIATION)

oughbred, Saddlebred, Standardbred, and Morgan. The horse stands approximately sixteen hands high, with an arched neck, deep chest and short back. The breed is now used as a pleasure and show horse.

tent pegging
A game in which contestants try at the gallop to spear one or more small wooden stakes embedded in the ground. Tent pegging began as an exercise among British cavalry units stationed in India in the nineteenth century.

terret
On a harness, a loop or ring on the saddle through which the reins pass.

test
(1) in dressage, a stipulated sequences of movements and transitions on which horses and riders are judged;
(2) in horse showing, an additional round of competition in horsemanship and other classes to give the judge further information on which to base his placements. Depending on the class, tests can include further work along the rail or over fences, executing certain patterns, and even answering oral questions posed by the judge. Also known as a ride-off.

tetanus
A severe, often fatal, bacterial infection marked by rigidity of muscles, especially of the head and face, a "sawhorse" stance, and convulsions. Also called lockjaw, tetanus most often is the result of a puncture wound that allows the bacteria to enter the body. Treatment includes tetanus antitoxin, sedatives, muscle relaxants, and intravenous fluids.

Tevis Cup Endurance Ride
The most famous 100-mile endurance ride in the United States, named for Lloyd Tevis (1824-1899) by his grandson Will Tevis, an early benefactor of the Ride. The trophy is awarded to the first rider to complete the 100 miles whose mount is "fit to continue." The ride takes place from Lake Tahoe to Auburn, California. Winning times over the past decade have been under 16 hours.

Thoroughbred
The breed closely associated with flat and steeplechase racing because of its superlative speed at distances over a quarter mile. All Thoroughbreds can trace their ancestries back to one or more of the three foundation sires: the Byerly Turk, Darley Arab, and Godolphin Barb, that were bred to native English mares in the seventeenth and eighteenth centuries.

Standing at approximate sixteen hands, the lithe and long-legged Thoroughbred is powerful and graceful in action or repose. In addition to its use as a racehorse, the Thoroughbred has achieved great success as a show hunter and jumper, foxhunter, dressage mount, and by contributions to the heritage of such breeds as the Standardbred, American Quarter Horse, Saddlebred, and the European Warmbloods.

thoroughpin
A swelling of the tendon sheath above the hock joint. Although the cause remains unknown, it may come from conformation problems. The treatment is anti-inflammatory medication.

three-day event
See combined training.

three-gaited
Of American Saddlebreds, able to move at the walk, trot, and canter. *Cf.* five-gaited.

three-point contact
In hunter-seat equitation, the rider's position in which the legs and seat are in contact with the horse. Also known as full seat. *Cf.* half-seat.

throat latch
(1) The portion of the body between the neck and the lower jaw bone;

Thoroughbred being exercised during a morning workout

(2) The bridle strap that buckles under a horse's throat. Its purpose is to prevent the bridle from slipping over the animal's head.

throttle
The throat, gullet, or windpipe.

throw-in
In polo, the "face-off" in which the referee tosses the ball onto the ground in front of the gathered players. A throw-in begins play at the start of each chukker and resumes play after some penalties.

thrush
An infection of the frog of the foot. Easily identified by the foul odor of a dark fluid discharge, thrush often results when a horse inhabits a dirty or damp stall or pasture. Treatment includes trimming the affected

Thrush

tissue, cleaning the foot, and better stable management.

thumps
A spasmodic breathing condition also known as synchronized diaphragmatic flutters. Occurring after strenuous exercise, it is characterized by convulsive twitching of the flanks. Treatment includes rest, administration of electolytes and water, and grazing (grass contains essential minerals to replace those lost in exercise).

tick
See rub.

tied at the knee
A conformation defect marked by visibly constricted tissue behind and below the knee. The condition restricts a horse's action.

tie-down
The Western term for a standing martingale.

tie up
To suffer severe muscle cramps, usually after unaccustomed exercise. *See* azoturia.

tight
In jumping, a take-off distance that is uncomfortably close to the fence; also known as deep. *Cf.* long.

timed event
Any competition, such as barrel racing, calf roping, or pole bending, in which the time to complete the course or otherwise finish the exercise will determine the order of finish.

timothy
A type of grass used as hay.

tobiano (tow-be-AN-o)
A Paint or pinto coat of primarily white with overlaid patches of color. *See* overo.

Tobiano

toe
The front portion of the foot.

toed-in.
See pigeon toed.

toed-out
See splay footed.

tolt
The comfortable running walk of the Icelandic Horse.

Tom Thumb
(1) a Weymouth bit with a low port, straight mouthpiece, and short cheekpieces. Only slightly more severe than a snaffle, the Tom Thumb, like other Weymouths and pelhams, is often used by people who think the look sets off a horse's head in an attractive way;
(2) a spur having a short neck.

tongue tie
In racing, a strap or tape bandage with which the horse's tongue is tied down, to prevent the animal from swallowing the tongue and choking.

top line
(1) The contour of a horse's back from withers to tail;
(2) The upper portion of a family tree that indicates the horse's paternal breeding. *Cf.* bottom line.

totalizator board (tote board)
In racing, the electronic display that gives up-to-the-minute odds and the amounts of money bet on the various wagering pools.

touch.
See rub.

tout (rhymes with "shout")   (From a Middle English word meaning "peek," as if spying to learn inside information about a horse's condition, training, etc.); a racetrack figure who claims to have advance information on a race and is eager to share it—for a price.

trace
In driving, one of the straps by which a horse is harnessed to a vehicle.

trace clip
A clipping pattern in which tracks along the belly, girth, and chest are trimmed. The horse is clipped where harness traces would come into contact with the animal, hence the name.

track
As a noun, (1) the path taken by the horse's feet, either individually or in pairs of the left or the right feet; *see* two-track;
(2) the path around a riding arena;
(3) a racecourse.
   As a verb, to move around a ring or arena. The phrase "track to the left" indicates moving in a counterclockwise direction.

trail horse
A Western horse show class in which horses are judged on their ability to deal with the varieties of obstacles found on an actual trail ride. Obstacles along the course might include a bridge to be crossed, rails laid out to form a T or L through which the horse will move at the walk or rein-back, and a mailbox that the rider will open while the horse stands quietly.

A trail horse class
(© WYATT MCSPADDEN/AMERICAN
QUARTER HORSE ASSOCIATION)

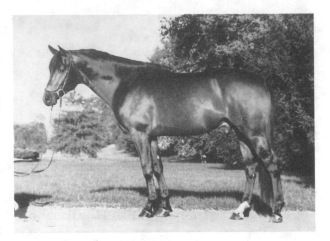

Trakehner
(© PAT GOODMAN/AMERICAN
TRAKEHNER ASSOCIATION)

trainer
The person who conditions and prepares horses for racing or showing or who educates a horse.

Trakehner (tra-KAIN-er)
(1) A Warmblood breed that originated during the early eighteenth century in an area that has been (according to the prevailing geographical boundary) eastern Germany or Western Poland. Infusions of Arabian and Thoroughbred blood contributed to the Trakehner's deep chest and strong back and legs. They are used primarily for show jumping and dressage;

(2) A combined training, cross-country obstacle composed of a post-and-rail fence set in a dry ditch.

trap
In driving, a light two-wheeled carriage.

travers (tra-VAIR)
A two-track oblique movement in which the horse's forelegs describe an outer track and his hind legs an inner track. *See* renvers.

tree
The frame of a saddle. A spring tree, usually found on jumping saddles, has metal strips that allow some flexibility, while rigid trees, such as those on dressage and Western saddles, are relatively inflexible.

trial
(1) In racing, an event in which eligible horses compete to determine the finalists in a nomination race;

170

A Western saddle tree

(© CHERRY HILL)

(2) A combined training competition that takes place over one or two days; also called a horse trial;

(3) A dressage competition.

tricolor

The familiar name for the three-colored prize ribbons awarded to a horse show division champion (blue, red, and yellow) or reserve champion (red, yellow, and white).

trifecta

In racing, a type of wager in which the bettor must select the first three finishers in exact order; also known as a "triple".

Trigger

The palomino ridden by the cowboy movie and television star Roy Rogers.

trip

Familiarly, a round in an over-fences horse show class.

Triple Crown

Collectively, the Kentucky Derby, Preakness Stakes, and Belmont Stakes races. Since the "youngest" of the races, the Kentucky Derby, was inaugurated in 1875, eleven Triple Crown winners have swept all three: Sir Barton (1919), Gallant Fox (1930), Omaha (1935), War Admiral (1937), Whirlaway (1941), Count Fleet (1943), Assault (1946), Citation (1948), Secretariat (1973), Seattle Slew (1977), and Affirmed (1978).

troika (from the Russian word for "three")

In driving, the traditional Russian carriage or sled pulled by three horses harnessed three abreast and controlled by four separate reins in the driver's hands, two for the center horse and one for each of the outside horses. The center horse trots, while the outer horses gallop.

Trojan horse

In Greek legend, the huge wooden horse built by the Greeks and left outside the walls of Troy during the Trojan War. When the curious Greeks hauled the horse inside the city, Greek soldiers who had been hiding inside the horse came out and opened the city's gates to allow other soldiers to enter. In the battle that followed, Troy lost the war.

trot

The two-beat gait in which the horse's feet move in diagonal pairs. The sequence of footfalls is left hind and right fore, then right hind and left fore. *See* jig, jog, long trot, and post.

The trot

(© CHERRY HILL)

tube
To insert a tube through a horse's nostril into its stomach to deliver medication; or, to hydrate the horse, water.

turnback
In cutting competitions, one of the riders who keep the herd together so that those cattle do not interfere with one being worked.

turn on the forehand
A change of direction in which the horse halts, then circles his hindquarters around his forelegs.

turn on the haunches
A change of direction in which the horse, while continuing to walk forward, circles his forequarters around his pivoting hind legs.

tush
The canine tooth of the horse. In mares this tooth is very small and usually does not break through the gums, but in males it is large and somewhat pointed.

twist
The portion of the saddle between the rider's thighs.

twisted wire snaffle
A snaffle bit with a corkscrew-shaped mouthpiece. The wider the corkscrew's spiral, the milder the bit's effect.

twitch
A restraining device that puts pressure on the horse's lip, used during a medical examination or treatment to distract the animal from the attention to another part of its body.

Using a twitch

two-point
See half seat.

two track
Any of the lateral movements in which the horse moves forward and sideways simultaneously, the animal's feet moving in separate but parallel paths. *See* half pass, renvers, travers.

typey; typie
A horse that conforms to the conformation standards of its breed and thus is the right "type."

undefended penalty shot
In polo, a penalty shot that the opposing team may not try to block. The player taking the shot has a clear chance at the goal. *Cf.* defended penalty shot.

undershot
A conformation defect in which the lower jaw extends beyond the upper jaw; also known as monkey-mouthed.

unicorn
In driving, a three-horse hitch with one leader and two wheelers.

United States Equestrian Team
The organization responsible for designating and training horses and riders for international competitions in dressage, driving, reining, show jumping, and three-day eventing.

United States Harness Association
The governing body of Standardbred racing.

United States Polo Association
Polo's governing body in this country.

unsoundness
An imperfection or physical condition, such as lameness, that restricts a horse's usefulness.

up
The direction away from the gate of a ring or arena. To jump up a particular line of fences is to start by jumping the fence closest to the gate and then head away from the gate. *Cf.* down.

up-down lesson
A lesson for beginning riders, so-called because of the "up-down up-down" instructions given for the basics of posting to the trot.

uveitis
See moon blindness.

vaquero (va-CARE-oh)
The Spanish word for cowboy. *See* buckaroo.

valet
In racing, the attendant who takes care of a jockey's equipment.

vaulting
A sport in which participants leap on and off a moving bareback horse and perform gymnastic maneuvers while standing, kneeling, or lying on the horse's back.

vehicle
The umbrella term for a wagon, cart, or coach pulled by one or more driving horses.

Venezuelan Equine Encephalomyelitis (VEE)
A highly contagious viral disease affecting the central nervous system. Occurring in warm climates but only very rarely in the United States,
its symptoms include fever, loose bowels, and severe disorientation. It is invariably fatal.

vertical
Any type of jump composed of a single element of width. *Cf.* oxer.

Vertical fence

vet check
Any of the mandatory physical examinations during a distance ride or a combined training event. Medical professionals assess the horse's condition with regard to its ability to continue in the competition. *See* CPR.

veterinarian
A doctor who treats animals.

Vetrap®
A type of elastic bandage used for medical treatment and to wrap legs for support.

view
In foxhunting, to spot a fox emerging from a covert.

view halloo!
In foxhunting, the attention-getting shout uttered by the first person to view the fox.

Visalia (vis-SAIL-ya)
A Western bell-shaped stirrup favored by calf ropers for its ease in dismounting.

voice
One of the rider's aids used to urge or soothe the horse. A cluck of the tongue or a kissing sound (jockeys call it "smooching") is the traditional signal to ask a horse to move forward or to encourage a moving horse to move faster. "Whoa" is the vocal signal to halt.

volte
In dressage, a circle measuring six meters in diameter.

voluntary withdrawal
The decision by a rider not to continue in a competition. The reason may be an injury or a substandard performance. *Cf.* elimination

wagonette
In driving, a four-wheeled vehicle with one seat facing forward and, behind it, two bench-like seats set lengthwise and facing each other.

walk
The slowest of the natural gaits. It is a four-beat gait, with the following sequence of footfalls: one hind foot, the fore foot on the same side, the other side's hind, and that side's fore.

walk on!
A direction to a horse to begin to walk. Of British origin, it is routinely used in driving and less often in other English disciplines.

walkover
In racing, a race in which only one horse takes part. The horse must complete the course, sometimes done at a walk, in order to be entitled to the purse.

walk-trot horse
A three-gaited American Saddlebred (as distinguished from the five-gaited variety).

wall
The hard supportive structure of the hoof.

walleye
A blueish eye surrounded by white. Although widely considered to be unattractive, it is not considered a conformation defect.

'Ware! (short for "beware")
In foxhunting, a warning of some sort of danger. For example, "'Ware hole!" alerts riders to a hole in the ground.

Warmblood
A type of sport horse that originated in Europe through the selective breeding of Thoroughbreds or Arabians (the so-called hot breeds) and draft horses (the coldbloods). The result produced such breeds as the Selle Français, Trakehener, Oldenburg, Hanoverian, and Swedish and Dutch Warmbloods. Originally created as cavalry horses, Warmbloods are now prized for dressage and show jumping.

warm-up
(1) In racing, a prerace slow gallop or canter to the starting gate;
(2) Any exercise intended to loosen up a horse for any further physical activity.

washy
In racing, broken out in a nervous sweat in the paddock or on the way to the starting gate.

way of going
Another term for action.

weanling
A foal that is no longer dependent on its mother's milk for nourishment.

weaving
A stable vice in which the horse rocks from side to side, often the result of boredom.

weedy
A thin body with little flesh, as if as thin as a weed.

weigh-in
In racing, the postrace procedure where the clerk of scales makes certain that each jockey carried the correct assigned weight.

weigh-out
In racing, the prerace procedure where the clerk of scales makes certain that each jockey will carry the correct assigned weight.

weight-for-age
In racing, a fixed scale of weights to be carried by horses according to age, sex, distance of race, and season of year.

weight pad
In racing, the pad worn under the saddle that holds the lead bars that make up the difference between the jockey's actual weight and the weight the horse has been assigned to carry.

well let-down
Having short hind cannon bones, considered an indication of strong hindquarters.

well-mounted
Riding a horse that is suitable for the rider's size and purposes.

Welsh
A native British pony now prevalent in the United States. Standing between 12.5 and 13.5 hands and usually gray in color, the Welsh is sturdy under saddle or in harness and a talented children's show hunter pony. Formerly known as the Welsh Mountain pony.

Western horsemanship
A horse show class in which the rider's stock-seat form and control are judged. Riders first individually ride a prescribed pattern that may include straight lines, curves, and circles, then work as a group at the walk, jog, and lope.

Western pleasure
A horse show class in which the horse's performance as an enjoyable mount is judged. Riders must hold the reins in one hand (and not switch hands during the class), nor can they touch their horses or tack with the free hand.

Western riding
A horse show class in which the horse is judged on the quality of gaits and especially on prompt and accurate lead changes. Contestants perform one of two preselected patterns that involve riding over or around a log and pylons.

A Western riding class
(© WYATT MCSPADDEN / AMERICAN QUARTER HORSE ASSOCIATION)

Westphalian
Some authorities consider the Westphalian Warmblood as a strain of Hanoverian horses that were bred in the German state of Westphalia. However, others consider Westphalians to be a distinct breed. In any event, the horses are used in dressage and show jumping.

Weymouth
The curb bit of an English double bridle.

wheat
A cereal of which the stalks are used as straw.

wheel
In racing, a bet in which one horse is combined in an exacta or trifecta with all other horses in the race, with that horse bet to win. That horse's winning means an assured payoff on the exacta or trifecta bet. A part wheel involves one horse with selected other horses; a back wheel involves choosing the horse that will finish second with multiple combinations with all the other horses bet to win.

wheeler(s)
In driving, the horse(s) hitched next to the vehicle. *See* leader(s).

whip
(1) A thin stick carried by the rider or driver and used to urge or correct a horse;
(2) The driver of a vehicle, so-called for the whip he or she carries;
(3) Short for whipper-in.

whipper-in
In foxhunting, a hunt staff member who keeps the hounds together as a pack; also known as whip.

white
(1) The color of an albino horse; all other "white" horses, no matter how colorless their coats appear to be, are properly described as gray;
(2) The color of the prize ribbon awarded for fourth place.

white line
The junction of the sole and the wall of the hoof. Horses that have foundered have a widened white line.

whoa (WOE, HOE)
The traditional vocal request to halt.

wind puffs
Swellings on the side of the tendon just above the fetlock. Cased by excessive stress on the joint, confinement after exercise, or faulty shoeing, wind puffs are treated by applications of ice, supportive bandages, and rest. Also known as wind galls.

windsucking
The stable vice of taking air into the lungs without biting onto anything (which distinguishes windsucking from cribbing).

winging
An undesirable movement, caused by poor conformation, in which the horse's legs swing inward and interfere with each other; also known as winging in or toeing in.

wings
Gatelike barriers on the sides of a jump that deter horses from running out at the obstacle.

winner's circle
In racing, the enclosure where winning horses are brought and where trophy ceremonies are held.

withers
The highest part of the back, where it meets the base of the neck. A horse's height is measured from the withers to the ground. *See* hand.

Withers

with the motion
See motion.

wobbles
The common name for foal atoxia, wobbles is a neurological condition caused by an injury to the vertebrae that produces muscle weakness and impaired coordination. There is no known cure.

wolf tooth
A premolar that is unnecessary for chewing and likely to interfere with the bit; the tooth is therefore routinely extracted before the horse begins its training.

working cow horse
A Western horse show class composed of two phases. In the first, the "dry work," the horse and rider execute a reining pattern. The horse then works a cow by first holding it at the end of the arena, then drives the cow along the arena fence in both directions and finally moves the cow into the middle of the arena and turns it in both directions.

working hunter
A horse show class or division in which the horse's jumping style over fences is judged. The term *working*, in the sense of performing, distinguishes these horses from conformation hunters. "Working" is also the division that follows second-year green. Fences may range in height from three feet six inches to four feet.

Working hunter class
(© WYATT MCSPADDEN/AQHA)

World Championships
Quadrennial international competitions held by the F.E.I. in dressage, driving, show jumping, and three-day eventing. As with the World Cup, locations of these events vary.

World Cup
Annual dressage and show jumping competitions under the aegis of the F.E.I. for which riders qualify throughout the year. Locations vary from year to year.

wormer
Oral medication that rids the horse of parasites. The medication can be administered in the form of paste or liquid. The word is used interchangeably with *dewormer*.

wrangler
The Western term for a ranch hand whose chores range from schooling horses to escorting dude ranch guests.

wrap
A general term for a lower-leg bandage worn for support and/or protection.

wrong lead
The incorrect lead at the canter, such as the left lead when circling clockwise. When done intentionally as a suppling and balancing exercise, it is called the counter-canter.

Xenophon (430 BC–355 BC)
Greek author of the first extant treatises on horsemanship. His "On The Art Of Horseman-ship" and "On Cavalry" suggested that trainers accomplish their goals through an understanding of the horse's mentality instead of using brute force.

Yabusame (ya-boo-SAH-me)
Classical Japanese horsemanship that includes shooting a bow-and-arrow at the gallop.

yearling
A horse between the ages of one and two.

yellow
The color of the prize ribbon for third place.

yielding
In racing, a turf surface having deep footing but without the presence of moisture. *See* soft.

yoiks! (pronounced "hoi" and shouted in a high-pitched voice)
In foxhunting, a cry of encouragement by the huntsman to the hounds. The word is thought to have come via Old French from the Latin word meaning "there!"

young entry
In foxhunting, young hounds that are not yet ready, whether by age or training, to join the hunt's pack.

zebra
The striped wild equine native to Africa. Some, but not many, zebras have been domesticated to the point of accepting a rider.

zebra dun
A dun with black stripes on its forearms.

References

The information in this section is included for reader reference. It is not intended as an endorsement or evaluation of any organization or company.

ASSOCIATIONS AND ORGANIZATIONS

Registries and Associations by Breed

Akhal-Teke

Akhal-Teke Registry of America
21314 129th Avenue, SE
Snohomish, WA 98296–7843
Tel: 425–485–4970
Fax: 360–668–4302

Andalusian

International Andalusian And Lusitano Horse Association
101 Carnoustie North, #200
Birmingham, AL 35242
Tel: 205–995–8900
Fax: 205–995–8966
Web address: www.andalusian.com

Appaloosa

Appaloosa Horse Club, Inc.
P.O. Box 8403
2720 West Pullman Road
Moscow, ID 83843–0903
Tel: 208–882–5578
Fax: 208–882–8150

International Colored Appaloosa Association, Inc.
P.O. Box 99
Shipshewana, IN 46565
Tel: 219–825–3331
Fax: 219–825–3331

Arabian

Arabian Horse Registry of America, Inc.
P.O. Box 173886
Denver, CO 80217–3886
Tel: 303–450–4748
Fax: 303–450–2841
Web address: www.theregistry.org

Arabian Sport Horse Association
6145 Whaleyville Blvd.
Suffolk, VA 23438–9730
Tel: 757–986–4486

International Arabian Horse Association/Half Arabian and Anglo-Arabian Registries
10805 East Bethany Drive
Aurora, CO 80014–2605
Tel: 303–696–4500
Fax: 303–696–4599
Web address: www.iaha.com

Cleveland Bay

Cleveland Bay Horse Society of North America
P.O. Box 221
South Windham, CT 06266–0221
Tel: 860–423–9457
Fax: 860–423–9457
Email: jescott@yahoo.com

Clydesdale

Clydesdale Breeders of the U.S.A.
17346 Kelley Road
Pecatonica, IL 61063
Tel: 815–247–8780
Fax: 815–247–8337

Cream Draft Horse

American Cream Draft Horse Association
2065 Noble Ave.
Charles City, IA 50616–9108
Tel: 515–228–5308

Dartmoor Pony

American Dartmoor Pony Association
203 Kendall Oaks Drive
Boerne, TX 78006
Tel: 830–249–8103
Fax: 830–249–7322

Dartmoor Pony Society of America
145 Upper Ridgeview Road
Columbus, NC 28722
Tel: 828–894–5672

Dutch Warmblood

Dutch Warmblood Studbook In North America, NA/WPN
609 E. Central
P.O. Box 0
Sutherlin, OR 97479
Tel: 541–459–3232
Fax: 541–459–2967
Web address: www.nawpn.org

Fell Pony

Fell Pony Society
Brougham Hall, Penrith
Cumbria CA10 2DE
England
Tel: 01768–891001
Fax: 01768–891001

Fjord

Norwegian Fjord Horse Registry
1203 Appian Drive
Webster, NY 14580–9129
Tel: 716–872–4114
Fax: 716–787–0497

Friesian

Friesian Horse Association of North America
P.O. Box 11217
Lexington, KY 40574
Web address: www.fhana.com

Galiceno

Galiceno Horse Breeders Association
Box 219
Godley, TX 76044–0219
Tel: 817–389–3547

Hackney

American Hackney Horse Society
4059 Iron Works Parkway, Suite 3
Lexington, KY 40511–8462
Tel: 606–255–8694
Fax: 606–255–0177
Web address: www.hackneyhorse.com/AHHS.html

Haflinger

American Haflinger Registry
4078 Broadview Road
Richfield, OH 44286
Tel: 330–659–2940
Fax: 330–659–2942

Hanoverian

American Hanoverian Society, Inc.
4067 Iron Works Parkway, Suite 1
Lexington, KY 40511–8483
Tel: 606–255–4141
Fax: 606–255–8467
Web address: www.hanoverian.org

Holsteiner

American Holsteiner Horse Association
222 East Main Street, #1
Georgetown, KY 40324–1712
Tel: 502–863–4239
Fax: 502–868–0722
Web address: www.holsteiner.com

Icelandic

United States Icelandic Horse Congress
38 Park Street
Montclair, NJ 07042
Tel: 973–783–3429
Fax: 973–783–0777

Lipizzan

Lipizzan Association of North America
P.O. Box 1133
Anderson, IN 46015
Tel: 765–644–3904
Fax: 765–641–1205
Web address: www.lipizzan.org

United States Lipizzan Registry
707 13th Street SE, Suite 275
Salem, OR 97301–4005
Tel: 505–589–3172
Fax: 503–362–6393
Email: USLRoffice@aol.com
Web address: www.lipizzan.com/uslr.html

Miniatures

American Miniature Horse Association, Inc.
5601 South IH 35W
Alvarado, TX 76009
Tel: 817–783–5600
Fax: 817–783–6403

American Miniature Horse Registry
81-B East Queenwood
Morton, IL 61550
Tel: 309–263–4044
Fax: 309–263–5113

Missouri Fox Trotting

Missouri Fox Trotting Horse Breed Association, Inc.
P.O. Box 1027
Ava, MO 65608–1027
Tel: 417–683–2468
Fax: 417–683–6144
Web address: www.mfthba.com

Morab

International Morab Breeders Association and Registry
S.101 W. 34628 Highway 99
Eagle, WI 53119–1857
Tel: 414–594–3667
Fax: 414–594–5136
Email: imba@morab.com
Web address: www.morab.com

Morgan

American Morgan Horse Association, Inc.
P.O. Box 960
Shelburne, VT 05482–0960
Tel: 802–985–4944
Fax: 802–985–8897
Web address: www.morganhorse.com

National Show Horse

National Show Horse Registry
11700 Commonwealth Drive, #200
Louisville, KY 40299–2344
Tel: 502–266–5100
Fax: 502–266–5806
Web address: www.nshregistry.org

Nez Perce Horse

Nez Perce Horse Registry
POB 365
Lapwai, Idaho 83540
Tel: 208–843–7333
Web address: www.nezpercehorseregistry.com

Oldenburg

International Sporthorse Registry and Oldenburg Registry North America
939 Merchandise Mart
200 World Trade Center
Chicago, IL 60654–1102
Tel: 312–527–6544
Fax: 312–527–6573
Web address: www.isroldenburg.org

Paint Horse

American Paint Horse Association
P.O. Box 961023
Fort Worth, TX 76161–0023
Tel: 817–834–2742
Fax: 817–834–3152
Web address: www.apha.com

Palomino

Palomino Horse Association
HC 63, Box 24
Dornsife, PA 17823
Tel: 570–758–3067

Palomino Horse Breeders of America
15253 East Skelly Drive
Tulsa, OK 74116–2637
Tel: 918–438–1234
Fax: 918–438–1232
Web address: www.palominohba.com

Paso Fino

Paso Fino Horse Association, Inc.
101 North Collins Street
Plant City, FL 33566–3311
Tel: 813–719–7777
Fax: 813–719–7872
Web address: www.pfha.org

Percheron

Percheron Horse Association of America
P.O. Box 141
Fredericktown, OH 43019–0141
Tel: 740–694–3602
Fax: 740–694–3604

Peruvian Paso

Peruvian Paso Horse Registry of North America
3077 Wiljan Court, Suite A
Santa Rosa, CA 95407–5702
Tel: 707–579–4394
Fax: 707–579–1038
Web address: www.pphrna.org

Pinto

Pinto Horse Association of America, Inc.
1900 Samuels Avenue
Fort Worth, TX 76102–1141
Tel: 817–336–7842
Fax: 817–336–7416

Quarter Horse

American Quarter Horse Association
P.O. Box 200
Amarillo, TX 79168–0001
Tel: 806–376–4811
Fax: 806–349–6401
Web address: www.aqha.com

Foundation Quarter Horse Registry
Box 230
Sterling, CO 80751
Tel: 970–522–7822
Fax: 970–522–7822

National Foundation Quarter Horse Association
P.O. Box P
Joseph, OR 97846
Tel: 541–426–4403
Fax: 541–426–4206

Rocky Mountain Horse

Rocky Mountain Horse Association
2805 Lancaster Road
Danville, KY 40422–9303
Tel/Fax: 606–238–7754

Saddlebred

American Saddlebred Horse Association
4093 Iron Works Parkway
Lexington, KY 40511–8434
Tel: 606–259–2742
Fax: 606–259–1628
Web address: www.saddlebred.com

Shetland Pony

American Shetland Pony Club
81-B East Queenwood
Morton, IL 61550
Tel: 309–263–4044
Fax: 309–263–5113
Web address: www.shetlandminiature.com

Shire

American Shire Horse Association
P.O. Box 739
New Castle, CO 81647–0739
Tel: 970–876–5980
Fax: 970–876–1977
Web address: www.shirehorse.org

Swedish Warmblood

Swedish Warmblood Association of North America
P.O. Box 788
Socorro, NM 87801
Tel: 505–835–1318
Fax: 505–835–1321
Web address: www.wbstallions.com/wb/swana

Tennessee Walking Horse

Tennessee Walking Horse Breeders' and Exhibitors' Association
P.O. Box 286
Lewisburg, TN 37091–0286
Tel: 931–359–1574
Fax: 931–359–2539

Thoroughbred

Jockey Club
821 Corporate Drive
Lexington, KY 40503–2794
Tel: 606–224–2700
Fax: 606–224–2710
Web address: www.jockeyclub.com

Trakehner

American Trakehner Association, Inc.
1520 West Church Street
Newark, OH 43055
Tel: 740–344–1111
Fax: 740–344–3225
Web address: www.americantrakehner.com

Warmbloods

American Warmblood Registry, Inc.
P.O. Box 127
Davis, CA 95617–0127
Tel: 530–757–1377
Fax: 530–756–0892
Web address: www.Americanwarmblood.com

American Warmblood Society
2 Buffalo Run Road
Center Ridge, AR 72027
Tel: 501–893–2777
Fax: 501–893–2779
Web address: www.americanwarmblood.org

Welsh Pony

Welsh Pony and Cob Society of America, Inc.
P.O. Box 2977
Winchester, VA 22604–2977
Tel: 540–667–6195
Web address: www.scendtek.com/wpcsa

Equestrian Organizations

American Association for Horsemanship Safety
P.O. Box 39
Fentress, TX 78622
Tel: 512–488–2220
Fax: 512–488–2319
www.law.utexas.edu/dawson/index.htm
Information on horsemanship safety and legal liability, provided by a not-for-profit corporation
dedicated to education on safety and training riding instructors in safe practices.

The American Driving Society
P.O. Box 160
Metamora, MI 48455
Tel: 810–664–8666
Fax: 810–664–2405
www.americandrivingsociety.org
Organization promoting the sport of driving both competitively and for pleasure.

American Endurance Ride Conference
11960 Heritage Oak
Suite 9
Auburn, CA 95603
Tel: 530–823–2260
Fax: 530–823–7805
www.aerc.org
A national governing body for long distance riding.

American Horse Protection Association
1000 29th Street, N.W.
#T-100
Washington, D.C. 20007–3820
Tel: 202–965–0500
Fax: 202–965–9621
Organization concerned with the welfare of wild and domestic horses.

American Horse Shows Association
4047 Iron Works Parkway
Lexington, KY 40511
www.ahsa.org
The national equestrian federation of the U.S., acting as the regulatory body for the Olympic and World Championship equestrian sports, as well as 18 other breeds and disciplines of competition. Web site lists rules of competition, competitor points and standings, and membership information.

American Riding Instructors Association
28801 Trenton Court
Bonita Springs, FL 34134
Tel: 941–948–3232
Fax: 941–948–5053
www.win.net/aria/
Provides listings of instructors certified by the organization.

American Vaulting Association
642 Alford Place
Bainbridge Island, WA 98110–4608
Tel: 206–780–9353
Fax: 206–780–9355
www.americanvaulting.org
Promotes vaulting in the United States. Web site has results, rules, photos, and membership information.

Certified Horsemanship Association
La Juan Skiver, Executive Director
5318 Old Bullard Road
Tyler, TX 75703
Tel: 800–399–0138
www.cha-ahse.org/aboutcha.html
A non-profit organization that evaluates and certifies riding instructors for risk management skills, teaching ability, horsemanship knowledge, and professionalism.

Fédération Equestre Internationale
Avenue Mon Repos 24
P.O. Box 157, 1000 Lausanne 5
Switzerland
Tel: 41 21 310 47 47
Fax: 41 21 310 47 60
www.horsesport.org
The international governing body of horse sports.

Masters of Foxhounds Association of America
Morven Park
P.O. Box 2420
Leesburg, VA 20177
Tel: 703–771–7442
Fax: 703–779–7462
www.mfha.com
The governing body of organized fox, coyote and drag hunting in the United States and Canada.

National Barrel Horse Association
NBHA—725 Broad Street
Augusta, GA 30901–1050
P.O. Box 1988, Augusta, GA 30903–1988
Tel: 706–722–7223
Fax: 706–722–9575
www.nbha.com
Promotes and oversees the sport of barrel racing.

National Cutting Horse Association
4704 Hwy. 377 South
Forth Worth, TX 76116
Tel: 817–244–6188
Fax: 817–244–2015
www.nchacutting.com
Promotes and regulates the showing of cutting horses. Sanctions most of the cutting events
   held in the United States and abroad.

National Reining Horse Association
3000 N.W. 10th St.
Oklahoma City, OK 73101–5302
Tel: 405–946–7400
www.nrha.com
The national governing body of the sport of reining.

North American Riding for the Handicapped Association
P.O. Box 33150
Denver, CO 80233
Tel: 800–369–7433
Fax: 303–252–4610
www.narha.org
Promotes and supports therapeutic riding for people with disabilities.

United States Combined Training Association
525 Old Waterford Road, N.W.
Leesburg, VA 20176
Tel: 703–779–0440
Fax: 703–779–0550
www.eventingusa.com
Web site has information and history on combined training, events calendar and results,
   forums/chat, links, and excerpts from the organization's magazine, USCTA News.

United States Dressage Foundation
P.O. Box 6669
Lincoln, NE 68506–0669
Tel: 402–434–8550
Fax: 402–434–8570
www.usdf.org
Dedicated to the promotion of dressage. Web site includes events calendar and links.

United States Equestrian Team
Pottersville Road
Gladstone, NJ 07934
Tel: 908–234–1251
Fax: 908–234–9417
www.uset.org
Selects, trains, equips, and promotes equestrians to represent the United States in the Olympics and other major international competitions.

United States Polo Association
4059 Iron Works Parkway
Lexington, KY 40511–8483
Tel: 859–255–0593
800–232–USPA
Fax: 859–231–9738
www.uspolo.org
Founded in 1890, this organization promotes the sport and coordinates and supervises national and international polo games.

INTERNET RESOURCES

General Horse Sites

Equine Info
www.equineinfo.com
Links to a variety of horse subjects.

Equisearch
www.equisearch.com
News, chat, equine products and services, and classified ads.

Hay.net
www.haynet.net
A wide range of horse-related links.

Horsesearch.net
www.horsesearch.net
An equestrian search engine.

The International Museum of the Horse
www.imh.org
Web site of the Kentucky Horse Park's International Museum of the Horse. On-line exhibits about the horse in history and art, breed information and photos, and links.

The National Sporting Library
www.nsl.org
Web site of the research center devoted to horse and field sports.

Horse Health

American Association of Equine Practitioners Online
www.aaep.org/ownereducation
Articles on a wide range of medical conditions and horse husbandry.

Animal Science—Horse and Mule Publications
muextension.missouri.edu/xplor/aguides/ansci/horses.htm
Veterinary, breeding, and nutritional information from the University of Missouri.

Equine Reproduction
www.equine-reproduction.com
Articles on breeding, including artificial insemination.

Hoofcare and Lameness
www.hoofcare.com
Equine foot and leg health.

The Horse
www.thehorse.com
On-line guide to equine health care.

World Equine Health Network
www.wehn.com
Veterinary and nutritional information from a variety of resources.

Activities and Special Interests

Arabian Horse Times
www.ahtimes.com
Arabian industry news and events, articles, message boards, and chats.

Appaloosa Web-Zine
www.cayusefreelance.com/webzine.html
On-line source for Appaloosa enthusiasts.

Barrelhorses.com
www.barrelhorses.com
Site devoted to barrel racing: news, show listings, information on finding a trainer or buying a
   horse, chat rooms, and merchandise.

The Draft Horse Journal
www.drafthorsejournal.com
On-line version of the draft horse magazine.

Endurance Net
www.endurance.net
On-line resource for endurance and long-distance equestrian sports.

Equijournal
www.equijournal.com
Focuses on American equestrian sports at the upper levels of competition.

The Equestrian Times
www.horsenews.com
Worldwide news coverage of the three Olympic disciplines: show jumping, dressage, and
   three-day eventing.

REFERENCES

Equine Image
www.equineimage.com
For fans of and creators of equine art.

The Gaited Horse
www.thegaitedhorse.com
On-line version of the magazine about gaited horses of all breeds.

Horsepull
www.horsepull.com
For enthusiasts of competitive pulling contests for draft horses.

QuarterHorses.com
www.quarterhorses.com
Classified ads, industry information, and advertising for the Quarter Horse and pleasure horse
    industries.

Trot-OnLine
www.trot-on.com/intro.html
Site devoted to driving, with articles and classified ads.

U.S. Event Horse
www.useventhorse.com
News, results, and classified ads for the eventing community.

Western States Trail Association
www.foothill.net/tevis/index.html
Official Web site for the Tevis Cup Endurance Ride.

Western Horseman
www.westernhorseman.com
On-line version of the Western riding magazine.

Women's Professional Rodeo Association
www.wpra.com
Organization for the female rodeo competitor, primarily barrel racers. Under the
    WPRA's umbrella is the Professional Women's Rodeo Association, which sanctions
    all-women's rodeos and events in which women compete in bareback and bull riding and
    calf roping.

Racing and Shows

The Bloodhorse
www.bloodhorse.com
Magazine of the National Thoroughbred Racing Association.

National Museum of Racing
www.racingmuseum.org
A mini-tour of the Saratoga museum, including the Hall of Fame and a trivia and games
section.

National Thoroughbred Racing Association
www.ntra.com
Current events and fan information for the racing industry.

Rolex Kentucky Three-Day Event
www.rk3de.org
A close-up look at the famous annual competition.

Thoroughbred Owners and Breeders Association
www.toba.org
Information for racing and non-racing thoroughbred owners.

United States Trotting Association
www.ustrotting.com
News, breed history, and other information on harness racing.

Commercial Sites

Acmepet.com
acmepet.petsmart.com/horse
Articles on horses, links to breed sites, and horse chat rooms and newsgroups.

ArenaWest Outfitters
www.arenawest.com
Site aimed at young Western riders, with merchandise, events calendar, and message
boards.

Bits and Bridles
www.bitsandbridles.com
New and used equestrian equipment.

The Blanket Shop
www.blanketshop.com
Custom horse blankets and saddle pads.

Books Equine
www.webpony.com/booksequine
An on-line bookstore for horse-related titles.

Cherry Hill's Web Site
www.horsekeeping.com
Information, links, and books from the author on riding and horse care.

HorseDirect.com
www.horsedirect.com
Site for buying and selling horses on-line.

Horse Health USA
www.pbshorsehealth.com
Medicine, supplements, equipment, and other products related to horse maintenance.

Leslie Desmond's Web Site
www.lesliedesmond.com
Articles, products, and links from the co-author of *True Horsemanship Through Feel*.

HORSE MERCHANDISE RETAILERS
(Catalog and On-line Shopping)

Back in the Saddle
570 Turner Drive, Suite D
Durango, CO 81303
Tel: 970–385–4575
www.backinthesaddle.com
Tack and apparel for pleasure and endurance riding.

Beval Ltd.
10 Park Avenue
Gladstone, NJ 07934
Tel: 800–524–0136
and
50 Pine St.
New Canaan, CT 06840
Tel: 800–783–PONY
www.beval.com
www.butetsaddle.com
Hunter/jumper tack and apparel.

Blue Ribbon Leather Co.
737 Madison St.
Shelbyville, TN 37160
Tel: 931–684–8799
Saddle-seat tack and apparel.

BMB
3100 S. Meridian Ave.
Wichita, KS 67217
Tel: 888–BMB–TACK
www.bmbtack.com
Emphasis on Western tack.

Chamisa Ridge
P.O. Box 23294
Santa Fe, NM 87502–3294
Tel: 800–743–3188
www.chamisaridge.com
"New age" dressage items and natural neutraceutical products.

Chick's
P.O. Drawer 59
Harrington, DE 19952
Tel: 800–444–2441
email: saddles@chicksaddlery.com
www.chicksaddlery.com
Primarily Western tack and apparel.

Dover Saddlery
41 Pope Rd.
Holliston, MA 01746
Tel: 800–989–1500
www.doversaddlery.com
Hunter/jumper, dressage, and combined training tack and apparel.

Horse Country
60 Alexandria Pike
Warrenton, VA 20186
Tel: 800–882–HUNT
www.horsecountrylife.com
Foxhunting and hunt racing tack and apparel.

Libertyville Saddle Shop
P.O. Box M
2121 Temple Dr.
Libertyville, IL 60048–4913
Tel: 800–872–3353
www.saddleshop.com
English and Western tack and apparel.

Meyer's
113 Walton Ave.
Lexington, KY 40508
Tel: 606–252–2004
email: carlmeyers@qx.net
Saddle-seat tack and apparel.

Miller Harness Co.
350 Page Rd.
Washington, NC 27889
Tel: 800–553–7655
Hunter/jumper tack and apparel.

Nasco
901 Janesville Ave.
Fort Atkinson, WI 53538
Tel: 920–563–2446
and
4825 Stoddard Rd.
Modesto, CA 95356
Tel: 209–545–1600
www.enasco.com
Riding, stable, breeding, and farrier equipment.

Pard's Western Shop
306 N. Maple St.
Urbana, IL 61802
Tel: 800–334–5726
www.pards.com
Western tack and apparel.

Riding Right
7301 SW Kable Lane
Suite 700
Portland, OR 97224
Tel: 800–545–7444
www.ridingright.com
Emphasis on dressage tack and apparel.

Shepler's
6501 W. Kellogg
Wichita, KS 67277
Tel: 800–835–4004
www.sheplers.com
Western tack and apparel.

State Line Tack Inc.
P.O. Box 935
Brockport, NY 14420
Tel: 800–228–9208
www.statelinetack.com
English and Western tack and apparel.

Tack in the Box
P.O. Box 158
Sublimity, OR 97385
Tel: 503–581–2935
www.tackinthebox.com
English tack and apparel.

Wiese Equine Supply
1989 Transit Way
Brockport, NY 14420
Tel: 800–869–4373
www.wiese.com
Riding and veterinary items.